Cyber Security for Educational Leaders

As leaders are increasingly implementing technologies into their districts and schools, they need to understand the implications and risks of doing so. *Cyber Security for Educational Leaders* is a much-needed text on developing, integrating, and understanding technology policies that govern schools and districts. Based on research and best practices, this book discusses the threats associated with technology use and policies and arms aspiring and practicing leaders with the necessary tools to protect their schools and to avoid litigation.

Special features include:

- A Cyber Risk Assessment Checklist and Questionnaire that helps leaders measure levels of risk in eight vital areas of technology usage
- Case vignettes that illuminate issues real leaders have encountered and end-of-chapter questions and activities that help readers make connections to their own practice
- Chapter alignment with the Educational Leadership Constituent Council (ELCC) standards
- An entire chapter on Copyright and Fair Use that prepares leaders for today's online world
- A Companion Website with additional activities, assessment rubrics, learning objectives, and PowerPoint slides

Richard Phillips is Assistant Professor and Program Coordinator of Curriculum and Instruction at Delaware State University, USA.

Rayton R. Sianjina is Chair of Education, Director of Graduate Education Programs, and Professor of Education and Instructional Technology at Delaware State University, USA.

Cyber Security for Educational Leaders

A Guide to Understanding and Implementing Technology Policies

**Richard Phillips and
Rayton R. Sianjina**

Routledge
Taylor & Francis Group

NEW YORK AND LONDON

First published 2013
by Routledge
711 Third Avenue, New York, NY 10017

Simultaneously published in the UK
by Routledge
2 Park Square, Milton Park, Abingdon, Oxon OX14 4RN

Routledge is an imprint of the Taylor & Francis Group, an informa business

Library of Congress Cataloging in Publication Data
Phillips, Richard, 1958- author.
   Cyber security for educational leaders : a guide to understanding and
   implementing technology policies / Richard Phillips, Rayton R. Sianjina.
      pages cm
   Includes bibliographical references and index.
   1. Educational technology—Security measures.   2. Cyberspace—Security
measures.   3. Computer security.   I. Sianjina, Rayton R., author.   II. Title.
   LB1028.3.P4745 2013   371.33—dc23

ISBN: 978–0–415–63196–9 (hbk)
ISBN: 978–0–415–63197–6 (pbk)
ISBN: 978–0–203–09621–5 (ebk)

Typeset in by Bell Gothic and Perpetua
RefineCatch Limited, Bungay, Suffolk

SUSTAINABLE
FORESTRY
INITIATIVE

Certified Sourcing
www.sfiprogram.org
SFI-00555
The SFI label applies to the text stock.

Printed and bound in the United States of America by
Walsworth Publishing Company, Marceline, MO.

"To be a philosopher," said Thoreau, "is not merely to have subtle thoughts, nor even to found a school, but so to love wisdom as to live, according to its dictates, a life of simplicity, independence, magnanimity, and trust."

We may be sure that if we can but find wisdom, all things else will be added unto us. "Seek ye first the good things of the mind," Bacon admonishes us, "and the rest will either be supplied or its loss will not be felt."

Truth will not make us rich, but it will make us free . . . Henry David Thoreau

This book is dedicated to the children of the authors as they "seek ye first the good things of the mind." Children remember your fathers as they raised you single handedly as single fathers. While it was a change, it was worth it.

Contents

Preface

PURPOSE OF THIS BOOK

Cyber Security for Educational Leaders is an educational leader's guide for understanding technology policies governing their schools and districts. In these days of data driven accountability, this book will help educational leaders understand how to implement technologies, as well as which ones to implement in their schools. Additionally this book will allow the reader to review existing policies and practices, and, finally, will help them measure the threats associated with these technology policies. In essence this book will guide the leader to setting an effective technology culture within their school or district. The book is formatted from an instrument developed and tested by the authors in school systems using educational leaders as participants. The instrument, the "Cyber Risk Assessment Checklist and Questionnaire Profile" measures levels of cyber risk in eight vital areas of technology usage. The administration of this instrument is equal to a field experience, as described in Chapter 11.

Cyber Security for Educational Leaders stands alone from other technology applications textbooks, first because it was formatted from a reliable instrument, second because it allows the reader (undergraduate, graduate or doctoral students, or practicing leaders) to develop an understanding of best policy practices for schools, and, finally, because the instrument allows for a field experience where a clear understanding of the policies governing the school or district are investigated. These chapters, activities, and vignettes will give the reader the knowledge and skills to protect their schools from cyber threats. The textbook is also accompanied by a companion website (www.routledge.com/cw/phillips) containing supplemental materials such as assignments, assessment rubrics, learning objectives, and chapter PowerPoint slides.

The text contains 14 chapters; the first relates to the technology gap while describing technology integration into instruction. Chapter 2 provides a strong foundational understanding into the Total Cost of Ownership (TCO) of school technology. TCO establishes the roots for understanding the basic principles of policies and how they interrelate. The TCO of school technology is the understanding into setting policies for your investment. Chapter 2 relates to technology integration into instruction. Chapters 3–10 are policy chapters from which learners (educational undergraduate and/or graduate students) can gain an understanding of the best policy practices to protect the organization from cyber threats. These areas include policies related to acceptable use, authentication, Internet usage, access, auditing, physical, analysis, and privacy. Each chapter examines best practices. Chapter 11 contains the Cyber Risk Assessment instrument and the instructions to administer it with a scoring guide. The remaining chapters are "hot topics" chapters. They are: Chapter 12 "Electronic Bullying," Chapter 13 "Electronic Sexual Harassment," and Chapter 14 "Basics of Copyright and Fair Use."

There are vignettes after each chapter to deepen contextual knowledge with practical knowledge. Additionally, the authors have aligned the chapters in *Cyber Security for Educational Leaders* with the Educational Leadership Constituent Council (ELCC) standards, the accrediting standards for educational leaders that fall under the National Council for Accreditation of Teacher Education (NCATE). We have created an ELCC chapter matrix providing a quick reference and alignment of each chapter. There are added activities at the end of each chapter that related to the ELCC standards.

CHANGING LANDSCAPES OF EDUCATION

In order to be competitive in the international economy, the country's governors signed a historic agreement years ago, in 1999, that established broad national educational goals. This agreement emphasized educational outcomes that would result in the production of an effective workforce. Glenna and Melmed quoting Louis Gerstner, CEO of IBM, said, "Information technology is the force that revolutionized business, streamlined government and has enabled instant communication and the exchange of information among people and institutions around the world" (Rand, 1995–1996) This report also highlights a variety of important findings and recommendations. Among the most important findings are the societal lessons from the early experiences. As a result, it's emphasized that, "a key role of federal, state, and local officials is to tap the experiences of these 'pioneer' schools that can increase the probability that continued investments in educational technology will be well used." These educational leaders clearly and succinctly articulate other important factors and considerations:

■ The current effective use and continued introduction of educational technology are components of broader efforts of school reform and effectiveness.

- The goal is to achieve equity in schools that serve poor, minority, and special needs populations.
- Technology Costs should be built into schools' budgets not just as one-time capital expenditures, but as recurring costs.
- The goal is for effectiveness in leadership advocacy for the adoption of technology.
- The consideration is to solve challenges such as equipping teachers to effectively "exploit" technology as well as providing them with a plentiful supply of high-quality content software.
- The aim is to create and deploy technology with lessons learned from the 'pioneer' schools. In this case, the authors brought several as they relate to this point.
- The objective is to develop and foster a more effective assistance organization. Rand Corporation reports on its experience that in order to transform schools you must reform the programs through organized assistance that is ongoing and timely.

TECHNOLOGY CHALLENGES

The days of paper, pencils, and chalkboards as tools for educating children appear to be dwindling as technology has become an integral part of education. The students of today's classrooms have come from, for the most part, a time of multimedia in their lives. Smart cell phones, iPods, Xboxes, and computers are a part of young people's daily lives. Education cannot be only two dimensional, a teacher lecturing, and children thoughtlessly recording the information, only to turn around and repeat what the teacher reported on test day. The future appears to have more technology incorporated into a general lesson plan; tools that if used wisely can enhance education and the ever increasing reliance upon test scores. But is just placing a computer in the room a 100 percent guarantee for a successful classroom, or are there other important factors to consider? A careful examination into the factors that lead to a successful use of technology must be done.

In an age where many U.S. public schools are facing budgetary problems and many buildings are in need of repair, does money appropriated towards technology make sense? Fix the roof, replace old worn out plumbing, or invest in 200 computers and expensive software; which choice is better for school districts to take? Research has shown the latter choice of spending money on technology is well worth the expenditure. During his last year of presidency, Bill Clinton earmarked an additional $25 million in his budget towards technology in schools. Research has shown that computers integrated into the classroom are paying dividends. According to a study released by Columbia University, in *TechKnowLogia* (MacKinnon, 2003), the use of educational technology in West

Virginia led directly to gains in K-6 students' reading, math, and language skills. Ideally, in a best-case scenario, the students will take the material learned from their teacher and expand their knowledge by using computer technology. At-risk students in the inner cities are benefiting from computer integration in the classroom. Language skills and reading comprehension skills are improving, as is retention.

So what is the key to successful computer technology in the classrooms? There are three crucial factors: (1) careful selection of software and appropriate use of it in the classroom; (2) on-going teacher training programs; and (3) computers that are up-to-date and in good working order. These factors combined with careful integration of material from the teacher lead to the best outcome.

Technology based programs have their doubters too. Some researchers have expressed a concern that so much emphasis on computer work will take away from the students 'interaction with each other as well as with the classroom teacher. Others have wondered if technology alone can account for improved test scores; or are there other factors? Unreliable computer systems can lead to slow response or other problems that frustrate students. Researchers have also shown concern that children could develop carpal tunnel syndrome after constant use of the computer.

Evaluation of technology in schools shows that there are great advantages, when used properly as well as drawbacks when not used properly. A three dimensional picture of the human heart beating on a computer is so much better than a picture in a book. Teachers must know when a lesson can be enhanced by use of technology, use it appropriately, and use it wisely. Teachers must develop a "technogogy" combining their technology and pedagogy and administrators must know how to evaluate its effects on student outcomes.

In the classrooms of the 21st century a dilemma may exist of properly integrating technology into the classroom. A well run school contains curriculum that maximizes a teacher's ability to interact with the students while using present day technologies to enhance his/her lessons. As reported on CNN Student News, "to produce those benefits, educators say that computer usage must be quality not quantity. Traditional lessons work, students engaged with the teacher as well as other students is crucial and technology can produce great benefits." In the same article a study points out that teachers should have the technological skills to use computers and the proper programs to enhance a student's education. The study also reported that 81 percent of fourth graders and 76 percent of eighth graders had math teachers with computer training. However most states offer additional training but only a few require teachers get updated computer training before they can get their teacher's license renewed. This is a dilemma for the school districts that expend large amounts of funds to the purchase of software and computers. Are they being used wisely and with proper accountability measures and control for this tremendous output of county funds? Another problem exists in terms of studying the effectiveness of the technology. Since the phenomenon of technology is constantly evolving in today's schools, how is the use of it being monitored for effectiveness? Long range studies are hard to find. All in all technology in the classroom if used wisely and appropriately is without a doubt a great teaching tool. Therefore, educational leaders need to set policies that are effective as guidelines for all users. This book allows for just that, understanding, maintaining, and enforcing sound technology policies. *Cyber Security for Educational Leaders* is the educational leader's guide to understanding technology policies.

INFLUENCES OF FORCES

In 2010, under the presidency of Barack Obama another reform act was attempted, titled "Race to the Top," or RTTT. RTTT is a four year grant that is part of the American Recovery and Reinvestment Act, or ARRA. Unlike the Title I funds under the No Child Left Behind (NCLB), every state and school district will not receive RTTT funds. States have to choose to apply and have to be chosen in order to receive funding for implementation of their proposed plans of action. Will this small detail make a difference in the success of students, because schools are not forced to participate? Purposes of this act include:

- Adopting standards and assessments that prepare students to be successful in college and the workplace and compete in the global economy.
- Building data systems that measure student growth and success and inform teachers and principals about how they can improve instruction.
- Recruiting, developing, rewarding, and retaining effective teachers and principals, especially where they are needed most; Turning around our lowest-achieving schools.

There are several requirements for states receiving RTTT funding. States must find substantial measurements of student and teacher growth. They must also adopt the Common Core Standards in math and English for planning and instruction and use those standards when creating assessments by the 2014–2015 school years. According to Lohman (2010), states must also show reform in the following four areas: "(1) enhancing standards and assessments, (2) improving collection and use of data, (3) increasing teacher effectiveness and achieving equity in teacher distribution, (4) turning around low achieving schools." If states receive the grant money, it may only be used towards programs that were outlined in their applications.

In addition to the RTTT grant, Investing in Innovation, or i3, is another source of funding for U.S. education. i3 is a $650 million dollar grant that is open to non-profit organizations, school districts, and higher education institutions through the American Recovery and Reinvestment Act (ARRA). According to the Department of Education website, applicants for this grant must show that they are creating or enlarging programs that will help close the achievement gap and help students in need through research and innovation. If an organization is awarded the grant they must show the following:

- They have had success in closing gaps in previous years.
- They have increased student progress and proficiency.
- Graduation rates have increased, and drop-out rates have declined.
- They have recruited and retained high quality teachers and administrators.
- They have a private sector investor that will match 20 percent of the grant.

As of September 2010, 49 grants have been awarded out of the 1,700 applications that were submitted. All of these reforms have been attempts to prepare American students for high achievement in reading, math, writing, and test scores. Although core subjects are critical areas, they are merely the tip of the iceberg of problems that prevent students from becoming successful. In a speech given by President Obama, he stated that the government's education goal is that by the year 2020, 60 percent of young adults will have an associate's or bachelor's degree. This can be a complicated goal. According to David Warlick of www.connectlearning.com, out of 100 ninth grade students, 67 will graduate on time, 38 will go on to college, 26 will remain in college as sophomores, and only 18 will graduate from college within six years. How will America reach its goal?

American educational leaders have begun to collaborate with educational leaders from other countries. In September 2010, leaders from several countries gathered in Vienna, Austria for the Organization for Economic Co-Operation and Development/ Centre for Effective Learning Environments conference: IMAGINE! Explore Radical Visions for Tomorrow's Schools. The OECD website states the conference had creative workshops that were hands on, as well as "keynote speakers and panel discussions involving visionaries, change agents, policy makers, architects, and planners." Some of the workshop topics included major events and future developments in education. The following themes were also explored during this convention:

- Managing resources and creating learning environments for the future;
- Ensuring that educational spaces meet the needs of students in the future;
- Future technology for educational environments;
- Creating partnerships with private sector investors as a strategy for financing education in the future.

The future of education in America is contingent upon many pertinent areas being addressed from inside the brick and mortared buildings to the local streets and cyberspace. Some of those areas include:

■ Instructional coaching in classrooms, before and after school for academic support;
■ Supporting professional development;
■ Educational leaders, administrators, and teachers volunteering and visiting children weekly to assess their needs;
■ Inviting them to various community programs;
■ Teaching life skills training and family counseling;
■ Raising funds to assist family within the community.

Administrators, educational leaders, parents, students, and community leaders must work together to develop policies that will strengthen teachers professionally while improving and supporting students' learning and life skills. The new face of education in America will address students' growth and learning from the inside out. Accelerated learning will take place through interactive multimedia resources, networking via the Internet, interactive television, satellites, and other technologies that are governed by policies. Society will call for greater educational accountability, at all levels. Schools will respond to the increasing diverse population, not just in the student population but teachers and administrators. Teachers, administrators, social and health services professionals, parents, and the larger community will support and collaborate with each other to address the needs of children. Students will be prepared to learn and compete globally.

ELCC Elements and Related Chapters

1. Standard 1.0: An education leader applies knowledge that promotes the success of every student by facilitating the development, articulation, implementation, and stewardship of a shared vision of learning through the collection and use of data to identify district goals, assess organizational effectiveness, and implement district plans to achieve goals; promotion of continual and sustainable improvement; and evaluation of progress and revision of plans supported by stakeholders.
   Related Chapters: 3, 5, and 7
2. Standard 2.0: An education leader applies knowledge that promotes the success of every student by sustaining a culture conducive to collaboration, trust, and a personalized learning environment with high expectations for students; creating and evaluating a comprehensive, rigorous, and coherent curricular and instructional program; developing and supervising the instructional and leadership capacity; and promoting the most effective and appropriate technologies to support teaching and learning.
   Related Chapters: 1, 3, and 6
3. Standard 3.0: An education leader applies knowledge that promotes the success of every student by ensuring the management of the organization, operation, and resources through monitoring and evaluating management and operational systems; efficiently using human, fiscal, and technological resources; promoting policies and procedures that protect the welfare and safety of students and staff; developing capacity for distributed leadership; and ensuring that time focuses on high-quality instruction and student learning.
   Related Chapters: 1, 2, 3, 4, 5, 6, 7, 8, 9, and 10
4. Standard 4.0: An education leader applies knowledge that promotes the success of every student by collaborating with faculty and community members, responding to diverse community interests and needs, and mobilizing community resources by collecting and analyzing information

pertinent to improvement of educational environment; promoting an understanding, appreciation, and use of the community's diverse cultural, social, and intellectual resources throughout; building and sustaining positive relationships with families and caregivers; and cultivating productive relationships with community partners.

Related Chapters: 2 and 3

5. Standard 5.0: An education leader applies knowledge that promotes the success of every student by acting with integrity, fairness, and in an ethical manner to ensure a system of accountability for every student's academic and social success by modeling principles of self-awareness, reflective practice, transparency, and ethical behavior as related to their roles; safeguarding the values of democracy, equity, and diversity; evaluating the potential moral and legal consequences of decision making; and promoting social justice to ensure individual student needs inform all aspects of schooling.

    Related Chapters: 1, 2, 3, 4, 5, 6, 7, 8, 9, 10, 11, 12, 13, and 14

6. Standard 6.0: An education leader applies knowledge that promotes the success of every student by understanding, responding to, and influencing the larger political, social, economic, legal, and cultural context through advocating for students, families, and caregivers; acting to influence local, district, state, and national decisions affecting student learning; and anticipating and assessing emerging trends and initiatives in order to adapt leadership strategies.

    Related Chapters: 2, 5, 11, 12, 13, and 14

7. Standard 7.0: An education leader applies knowledge that promotes the success of every student in a substantial and sustained educational leadership internship experience that has field experiences and clinical practice within a setting and is monitored by a qualified, on-site mentor.

    Related Chapter: 11

    (NCATE (2012) *ELCC Elements*. Retrieved September 26, 2011, from http://aims.ncate.org/ProgRev/Agreements/Form391.pdf)

Matrix Elcc Elements and Related Chapters

ELCC	Ch1	Ch2	Ch3	Ch4	Ch5	Ch6	Ch7	Ch8	Ch9	Ch10	Ch11	Ch12	Ch13	Ch14
Standard 1.0	✓		✓		✓		✓							
Standard 2.0	✓		✓			✓								
Standard 3.0	✓	✓	✓	✓	✓	✓	✓	✓	✓	✓				
Standard 4.0		✓	✓											
Standard 5.0		✓	✓	✓	✓	✓	✓	✓	✓	✓	✓	✓	✓	✓
Standard 6.0		✓			✓						✓	✓	✓	✓
Standard 7.0											✓			

Acknowledgments

I wish to thank members of Delaware State University Doctoral Program of Studies who assisted in the research for this publication of best practices in cyber policies among educational leaders. Without their contributions this book would fall short.

Chapter 1

Introduction

KEY CONCEPTS
Leadership
CAI, CMI, CEI

OBJECTIVES
1. Describe the technology gap.
2. Match the related technology gap with emerging technologies.
3. Identify the leadership styles.
4. Define CAI, CMI, CEI.

RELATED ELCC STANDARDS
Standard 2.0
Standard 3.0
Standard 5.0

INTRODUCTION

Understanding the technology gap will help school leaders set policies that will protect both the organization and its users. Has technology divided educators between the technology-wise and the technology neophytes? Literature shows the technology gap plays a significant role within organizations and human resources management decision-making. The "technology gap" reported by the Maryland State Department of Education was formed during a period from 1992 to 2002 and reflects the rapid growth of computers in schools. An article in the *Journal of Technology and Teacher Education* (JYATE) described the digital divide as a technology gap in the following ways: it exists between new college graduates with less than 5 years of teaching experience and teachers with 5 years experience or more. The determining factor in the gap is between those teachers who integrate technology into instruction and those who don't have a clue how to because they lack the "necessary knowledge and skills" (Howard & Pope, 2002, p. 1). Across the nation school districts are making attempts to "bridge the technology gap" that exists between older, seasoned teachers and newer, more recently hired teachers (p. 1). Therefore, it is sound to recognize that school technology policies across the nation are in need of constant updates.

A growing number of children are becoming technologically smarter and quicker than many of their teachers, and although changes are being made in teacher training, children are progressing faster when it comes to technology. In the article, "National educational technology standards: raising the bar by degrees" in the online publication, *Info Today*, Bennett (2003) stated:

> There is a growing gap between the educational experience of a child who has access to various forms of technology with a tech-savvy teacher and children who have the gadgets and a teacher who doesn't know how to use them or has no gadgets. (p. 1)

Bennett explained the need to stimulate children in the classroom by addressing several individual child learning styles. Bennett referenced children having home computers, Nintendo games, Xbox, PlayStation, Droid, cell phones, and other sophisticated electronic devices that provide technological stimulation never before experienced by children. Teachers are challenged to compete with ever-changing technologies appearing in the classroom as they attempt to stay current with their students. Older educators, not as techno savvy as their students, are becoming more frustrated in classrooms as students disengage from time-honored methods of instruction. Bennett suggested national technology standards are needed in teacher training programs to bridge the technology gap between students and teachers. However, technology changes so rapidly that staff development attempts cannot educate teachers fast enough for them to understand and integrate new innovations and methods in the classroom before the technology has moved forward to present even newer challenges. Your authors have observed new technology gaps appearing and believe these gaps are cyclical with emerging technologies. Leadership plays a critical role in staff development and leaders must understand technology policies to support the culture of teaching and learning within their district or building. What are effective leadership styles and what knowledge do these effective leaders need to possess with emerging technologies?

LEADERSHIP

One of the more difficult tasks of being a school leader is engaging followers to impact students' learning (Robinson, 2007). According to Wu (2006), leadership is a phenomenon that has been studied extensively. Many theorists have provided various connotations for leadership (Offerman, Kennedy, & Wirtz, 1994; Stewart, 2006). Johnson (2001) makes the distinction between leader and follower in his writing regarding leadership, "Leadership is the exercise of influence in a group context . . . leaders are change agents engaged in furthering the needs, wants, and goals of leaders and followers alike" (p. 6). In contrast, Johnson offers a definition of the role of the follower. He writes, "Important follower functions include carrying out group and organizational tasks, generating new ideas about how to get jobs done, engaging in teamwork, and providing feedback" (p. 6).

An additional challenge that faces school leaders is to produce graduates that are able to be productive citizens in our society (Interstate School Leaders Licensure Consortium, 2008). Yell, Drasgow, and Lowery (2005) write the following regarding the government's role in education:

> The federal government's role in education has been an important one, often because it provides funds to assist states in crucial areas such as educating economically disadvantaged children and youth. The federal role has evolved from one in which the government primarily provided federal assistance to the states to one in which the federal government is holding states accountable for improving learning outcomes and achievement for all students. (p. 130)

The focus on instructional leadership has been renewed by the expectations of competing in a global marketplace and increasing student achievement (Gray, 2009). According to the U.S. Department of Education (2002), "International comparisons such as the Third International Mathematics and Science Study show middle and high school students in America performing at or below the average level" (p. 24). Brewster and Klump (2005) write, "The instructional leadership model attempts to draw principals' attention back to teaching and learning, and away from the administrative and managerial tasks that continue to consume most principals' time" (p. 5). According to Stewart (2006), "Instructional leaders focus on how administrators and teachers improve teaching and learning" (p. 4). Kruger, Witziers, and Sleegers (2007) believe instructional leaders are characterized by the number of activities that are positively connected to student achievement, such as "emphasis on basic subjects, coordination of instructional programs, and orientation towards educational development and innovation" (p. 2).

Conversely, the National Association of Elementary School Principals (NAESP) (2008) notes that "effective principals are transformational" (p. 1). NAESP (2008) highlights five attributes of an effective administrator:

> Effective principals look at data and analyze trends, gaps, and insights. Effective principals understand the job requires new levels of public relations

and better marketing of school goals and achievements. Effective principals create conditions and structures for learning that enable continuous improvement of performance not only for children, but for adults, too. Effective principals must be the lead learners in their schools. Effective principals are caring advocates for the whole child. (p. 2)

According to Hallinger (2003), "Transformational leadership focuses on developing the organization's capacity to innovate rather than focusing specifically on direct coordination, control, and supervision of curriculum and instruction" (p. 330). Transformational leadership involves the transformation of followers' and leaders' attitudes and beliefs. It requires the assessment of followers' needs and treating them equally as human beings (Northouse, 2001). Hopkins (2001) refers to the transformational leadership style as one where the leader tries to change the perception and the culture of the organization. The ultimate goal of a transformational leader is to transform the state of mind of the followers (Hopkins, 2001). Stewart (2006) writes, "Transformational leaders focus on restructuring the school by improving school conditions" (p. 4). Gunter (2001), referring to transformational leadership, indicates that the intention is to find the link between the influence of administrators, as leaders, on followers' behavior and on student learning outcomes.

Transactional leadership emphasizes the exchange relationship between the leader and subordinates. This leadership style is focused on leadership that encourages subordinates' work performance through the use of rewards and recognition. This leader works within the structural framework of the organization and reinforces the bottom line while maximizing the organization's efficiency and in this case they attempted to reach the targeted educational goals. There is a strong emphasis on the relationship between the leader and subordinates that allows for alignment within the organizational culture to share the mission and goals.

Whether one is an instructional, transformational, or transactional leader of a district or building the responsibilities remain the same. Student achievement is the number one outcome under the microscope and understanding the how of technology integration will allow all the stakeholders to buy into and support technology incentives in this century. Student achievement can only be achieved through effective teaching and learning through the integration of technology. And while technology plays a key role in teaching and learning there are several forms of integrating technology into teaching and learning which leaders must be aware of to effectively make informed decisions.

CAI, CMI, CEI

In this century, there are three identifiable forms of technology integration that are used for teaching and learning, and can be gained through educational staff

4

development. It is extremely important that educational leaders understand the three ways of integrating technology into instruction. They are described by two educational gurus Kirkpatrick and Cuban (1998) in *Techno Quarterly*. Cuban and Kirkpatrick asked "Are teachers both the problem and the solution?" (p. 1). The question was not facetious. "We stress that policymakers, practitioners, and parents need to know what they want to achieve with technologies, be familiar with research findings on computer assisted instruction (CAI), computer managed instruction (CMI), and computer enhanced instruction (CEI), and connect their aims to what is known" (p. 2).

> In education, technological based methods are described in the following ways:
>
> CAI (computer-assisted instruction) refers to computer programs that provide students with drill-and-practice exercises or tutorial programs.
>
> CMI (computer-managed instruction) refers to programs that evaluate and diagnose students' needs, guide them through the next step in their learning, and record their progress for teacher use.
>
> CEI (computer-enhanced instruction) provides less structured, more open-ended opportunities that support a particular lesson or unit plan. Use of the Internet, word processing, graphing, and drawing programs are examples of CEI. (p. 5)

By understanding the three identifiable forms of technology integration used for teaching and learning policymakers, practitioners, and parents know what is to be achieved in the classroom with technologies. Furthermore, by understanding the technology gap, educational leaders can set sound and relevant technology policies. Together with best practices these are the foundations of sound technology integration in our schools.

CONCLUSION

In this chapter you gained an understanding of technology regarding the ever-changing environment school leaders face. While effective leadership styles were also addressed there is a need to understand different forms of instructional methods, namely computer assisted instruction (CAI), computer managed instruction (CMI), and computer enhanced instruction (CEI), to enhance an understanding of how technology is integrated into instruction.

In the remaining chapters, we provide information so educational leaders can develop a "technogogy," combining knowledge of technology and pedagogy. The next chapter will address best practices regarding the total cost of ownership of technologies and the variables to consider when making purchases and technology upgrades for schools or districts.

QUESTIONS

1. Identify and explain one of the three forms of technology integration being used in your school.

2. List 5–10 areas of technology gaps and create a professional development to close these gaps.

3. How does leadership affect technology in teaching?

VIGNETTE CHAPTER 1   Hurdles

PS 187 is a public school located in an inner city school district. Most of the teachers have 10 years or more teaching experience, and only 10 percent have 5 years experience or less. Ms. Howard is the new principal at PS 187 and was promoted from within the school system.

Ms. Howard is a young principal with her Ed. D. in educational leadership and a master's degree in educational technology. She has 10 years of teaching experience in the classroom. She describes herself as an instructional leader, not a transformational or transactional leader. As an administrator, Ms. Howard believes in improving teaching and learning. Her main focus is on the integration of technology in the classroom.

During her first year as principal, she noticed problems and expressed her concerns to the Superintendent of Schools:

> Technology in PS 187 is lacking. There is little to no integration of technology into instruction. One problem is that the school building has a poor infrastructure to support many computer users. There is not sufficient electric power, not enough bandwidth, and one computer support person is shared between five schools. The problems are a result of poor planning, budget cuts and a growing gap between the experience of young teachers with technology and the lack of experience of older teachers.

During her second year as principal, Ms. Howard organized the School Improvement Team (SIT) to come up with a plan. They met with the Rotary Club, several business and industry leaders in the school district, the PTA, and various local government agencies to determine their level of support and commitment to technology in education. She found that many of the school's past graduates were unprepared and lacked the basic technology skills to compete in the local workforce. Most of the students worked in low paying, labor-related jobs and fast food. Many students had difficulties with college entrance exams. Other students deferred to the military.

With the SIT committee, Ms. Howard created a school improvement plan and timeline listing all the supporting stakeholders and their commitments in a methodical and logical manner. She found support to repair the infrastructure, business and community funding to purchase some technologies like Smart boards and ELMO readers, and a low-cost contractor to help with computer repairs when needed. She even found support from the cable company with bandwidth since the school was already wired with cable.

Over time, the SIT committee and the district curriculum specialist changed several programs and courses to integrate technologies into instruction and meet the needs of the business community. Finally, graduating students would be better prepared and more marketable.

The final hurdle was to close the technology gap with staff development. Teachers needed to be trained in how to use technologies, how to plan and instruct with technologies, and how to assess with technologies. Ms. Howard conducted a technology survey and measured levels of competency in the area of technology with a self-reporting Likert scale. As expected, the results indicated that younger teachers were more proficient than older teachers in the use of technology. She utilized her younger teachers to organize ongoing staff developments in place of routine after school staff meetings.

Mr. Horn, one of the older teachers with little technology experience, filed a complaint with the union representative because he felt that his contract was being violated in terms of required afterschool activities. The complaint focused on required additional unscheduled work and the lack of monetary compensation for additional hours of employment. When calculated for the entire teaching staff, the cost for one additional hour was estimated to be $2200 a week. Ms. Howard had scheduled 26 hours of additional afterschool staff developments. The union was threatening to sue since the cost was exceeding $57,000 in lost wages.

Many of the teachers who were initially supportive of staff development were balking because money was becoming an issue. Staff development in technology was the last big hurdle to jump at PS 187. Now, it seemed like faculty members were jumping ship one at time.

QUESTIONS

1. Discuss your understanding of the technology gap.

2. Make a list of the areas in your school where the use of technology in instruction could be improved.

ACTIVITY

1. In small group discussions identify from the list of stakeholders below the individuals that are affected by the dilemma in the vignette and brainstorm ways they can affect change.

2. How do they communicate and in what forum?

3. Discuss your school or district's written plan of action for this problem, if one exists.

4. Identify any resources that could be utilized to resolve this dilemma.

5. Have one person in your group take notes and share your group's findings in front of the class after the discussion.

6. Organize the consensus.

Outside Government Agencies	Outside Technology Professionals
Parents	Crisis Team
Principals	Outside Private Agencies
Staff	School Lawyers
Students	Counselor
Superintendent	School Board
Teachers	Media (TV, Radio, Internet)
Technology Personnel	State's Attorney

Chapter 2

Total Cost of Ownership

KEY CONCEPTS
Equipment costs
Operation and maintenance costs
Disposition costs
Non-operational costs

OBJECTIVES
1. Describe the Total Cost of Ownership and evaluate the estimated costs.
2. Match the related costs under the categories internal, external, tangibles, and intangibles.
3. Identify the long-term and short-term cost in owning technologies.
4. Identify operation and maintenance costs, equipment costs, disposition costs, and non-operational costs for the Total Cost of Ownership in the school or organization.

RELATED ELCC STANDARDS
Standard 3.0
Standard 4.0
Standard 5.0
Standard 6.0

INTRODUCTION

Today, a best practices approach to Total Cost of Ownership (TCO) is grounded in the theoretical framework of the Gartner Group. Understanding the TCO is essential for educational leaders to plan, budget, and manage school-based technologies. Gartner (2002) defined TCO as "a comprehensive set of methodologies, models, and tools to help organizations better measure, manage, and reduce costs and improve overall value of IT investment" (p. 4). In an Educase Center for Applied Research (ECAR) publication (2004) entitled *Total Cost of Ownership: A Strategic Tool for ERP Planning and Implementation*, it was stated that "Gartner originated the TCO concept about 15 years ago and has been the leading advocate for its use in IT as a major developer of TCO methodological tools and a contributor to the research literature on the topic" (p. 3). However, according to Gartner Applied Research e-Learning Center (2008), "the Total Cost of Ownership was first developed in 1987 by Bill Kirwin as a means of clearly and reasonably addressing the real costs attributed to owning and managing IT infrastructure in a business" (p. 1).

Additionally, TOC methodologies are derived from "neoclassical economics" (Wikipedia, 2012). "Neoclassical economics is conventionally dated from William Stanley Jevon's *Theory of Political Economy* (1871), Carl Menger's *Principles of Economics* (1871), and Leon Walras's *Elements of Pure Economics* (1874–1877)" (p. 2). Regardless of the evolutionary path TCO followed, it is evident that "TCO is a means for understanding and controlling the risk associated with implementing and ERP (Enterprise Resource Planning)" (ECAR, 2004, p. 2). Further, Gartner (2004) stated, "TCO is a means for understanding and controlling risk" (p. 5).

In previous research, the following cost elements were constantly highlighted by top researchers as being the main cost factors in technologies. They were: (a) purchase price, (b) installation costs, (c) financing costs, (d) commissioning costs, (e) energy costs, (f) repair costs, (g) upgrade costs, (h) conversion costs, (i) training costs, (j) support costs, (k) service costs, (l) maintenance costs, (m) downtime costs, (n) safety costs, (o) productivity costs, (p) risk costs, and (q) disposal costs (Gartner, 2004). With reference to educational technology, TCO is a financial estimate of equipment costs that assists the enterprise manager to determine direct and indirect costs of major capital expenditures. Indirect costs are administrative expenses not directly attributable to the technology purchase or technology operation. Referred to as "overhead costs," they include technology support, electrical costs, and administrative costs such as insurance. Direct costs would include equipment acquired for and directly attributable to the execution of a project. TCO is often underestimated when calculating the costs of infusing technology in educational initiatives. Estimates of costs above and beyond the actual equipment purchase lie between 10–25 percent of total cost. When considering an educational technology purchase, the savvy IT specialist needs to factor in four cost categories: equipment cost, operation and maintenance cost, equipment disposition cost, and non-operational costs.

Gartner stated, "The identification and measurement of direct and indirect costs are a critical requirement of TCO analysis" (p. 5). Direct costs are tangible expenditures such as "servers, peripherals, and networks, including capital, fees, and labor in each area" (p. 5). Indirect costs include "downtime and services to the end user" and "are difficult to identify or measure" (p. 5). A new emerging indirect cost to reduce risk is cyber insurance. No mention was made in TCO studies of cyber costs associated with risk. In fact, cyber risk management is considered an emerging field. Some school districts are self-insured while others have contracted with providers. Whatever the case may be, risk management aims to reduce the loss of data and equipment real threats. These threats are addressed collectively in each chapter.

For many principals, teachers, and students, the concept of "technology in the classroom" and its related applications is perhaps a little deceptive. Stakeholders question what could be so expensive about a couple of computers and a printer. Likely, the only people not deceived are the district's business manager and technology specialist. They realize the "real" cost of technology is a multitude of expenses that are incurred with "a couple of computers" in the classroom. The electricity that runs the computer, the cables that connect the computers, the tables to set the technology upon, the Internet access to let the students explore the global nature of the Internet are all expenses considered part of the TCO.

EQUIPMENT COSTS

From the start, equipment cost factors can be complicated. Cost of high-performance technology aside, the IT specialist has to decide between owning the equipment and/or leasing the equipment and to determine which would be more cost effective to the organization. Purchasing equipment that has a 3–5 year effective life span may be appealing if the specialist assumes the equipment will be replaced when it reaches end of life. However, for budgetary reasons, the equipment may be required to be in operation for 10 years. The IT specialist needs to factor in the costs of operating diminished-capacity equipment running at diminished effectiveness. Would leasing equipment with a guarantee of updating technology at the end of the leasing period be the smart alternative? Even when leasing, additional costs will be involved in moving out the old technology and installing newer technology. The IT specialist must calculate the economic gains and losses of each scenario and determine which would better serve the organization in the short term as well as the long term.

Some of the often forgotten equipment costs are peripheral equipment expenditures that are necessary for technology operations. This includes the cost of racks for switches, hubs, and other equipment that holds the operational technology, as well as the installation of electrical components to power the racks. Operational technology can include wired and wireless routers, servers for connectivity, email and video, software and memory for system backup and protection, RAID and various memory technologies, and technology management/automation software.

OPERATION AND MAINTENANCE COSTS

When calculating TCO for new technology, operation and maintenance costs would include the cost of: (a) wiring and interconnectivity, (b) maintenance of the technology warranty and possibly an extended warranty, (c) software and software licensing, (d) Internet carriage, Internet installation, and Internet maintenance, (e) electricity to run the technology being purchased, (f) installation of the technology and installation of any associated operations (installing software and testing), (g) daily maintenance and trouble-shooting, and (h) upgrading equipment, operating systems (OS) updates, software updates, interconnectivity updating, and the cost of bandwidth. In short, any costs that contribute to the new technology startup and long-term use would need to be included.

The cost of electricity to run the equipment and keep it cool is often a forgotten expense. The IT specialist needs to calculate the per-hour cost of running a typical computer tower, running its accompanying monitor, and running the servers and routers that maintain the system. The hourly cost would be multiplied by the number of computers in the system, and then multiplied by the number of hours that the system will run at full power over a period of a week. The results would be an approximate cost of power. In addition, the cost of running the system at reduced electrical usage in the overnight hours must be added to correctly calculate a total electrical usage for technology over an average year.

In the past 10 years, security management has become a critical component of IT systems operation and, depending on the size of the organization and the required level of security, it can be a significant factor when calculating TCO. This will be addressed in detail in later chapters. Maintaining system security requires specialized software, specialized monitoring equipment, and specialized staff members. IT system security management requires: (a) maintaining an accurate inventory of technology, (b) an accurate accounting of both potential system threats and incurred system threats, (c) OS system patch management, (d) consistent client and information cleanup and deletions, (e) consistent monitoring for virus outbreaks, (f) monitoring unauthorized access attempts, (g) monitoring hacking-related and Malware attacks, and (h) management of compliance with state and federal laws and standards. Again these concepts will be addressed in later chapters.

DISPOSITION COSTS

Disposition costs would include the peripheral costs of operating the new technology. Computer tables and computer chairs would be considered disposition costs. The cost of: (a) appropriate lighting, (b) lighting installation, (c) installing electrical outlets for the area where the new technology will be housed, (d) the square footage for the new technology area, (e) climate control for the new technology area, (f) peripheral technology for the new technology area (projector, Smart board, whiteboard, LCD screens), (g) physical computer lock-down, and (h) installation and maintenance of a security system for the new technology are all examples of the disposition costs that need to be calculated into the TCO. Installation of a new lab in a room that has a water sprinkler system is also a requirement and may represent an additional cost.

NON-OPERATIONAL COSTS

Non-operational costs can be defined as costs that are necessary, but not directly connected, to the operation of the new technology. One of the major non-operational costs that educational systems tend to neglect when considering TCO is training. The training needs include hardware and software training for the IT specialist, hardware and software training for the teachers and instructors, and hardware and software training for the end-users, the students. Non-operational costs often include peripheral business and administrative costs necessary to the overall technology program. Insurance is an example. Some federal, state, and private granting agencies require insurance to protect against theft, damage, and catastrophic loss.

As a business organizational component, technology also needs to be audited and inventoried on an annual basis requiring non-technical accounting personnel. IT specialists need to calculate and predict the cost of unexpected down time in the case of electrical, technological, or other catastrophic failure and the potential cost of temporarily renting or leasing technology to maintain operations. At some time in the future technology will need to be replaced, whether purchasing or leasing. Calculating the cost of replacement is often ignored in TCO. Replacement requires man hours, transportation, and disposal costs that need to be paid to make room for new technology.

The major implications that can be drawn from the available literature indicate the TCO is a major factor when considering technologies. School leaders are facing challenges as never before to hire and develop technologically prepared educators to meet the needs of techno-savvy children. With No Child Left Behind (NCLB) and Race to the Top (RTTT) compliance issues as a background, technology has become the driving force behind instruction, assessment, and staff development decisions. Best practices policies are needed to govern both organizations and users; thus, policies set the cultural environment of an organization and can provide a standard set of rules with which to determine how technology is managed and used for educational outcomes.

CONCLUSION

Determining the TCO for an organization's IT is a strategic evaluation process by which educational institutions and businesses can fully understand the direct and indirect costs associated with implementation, operation, and replacement of cyber technologies. In this chapter, you gained an understanding into technology regarding planning and applying principles of the TCO. The next chapter will address best practices regarding the first policy known as the "acceptable use policy" which governs the use of electronic equipment and protects the district, the school, the employee, and the student. The chapter sets the stage and identifies use and abuse of technologies.

QUESTIONS

1. What are the total costs of ownership methodologies? Explain.

2. How do direct and indirect costs effect technology planning?

3. Make a list of all the disposition costs and non-operational costs of your organization.

4. Compose a policy to effectively manage indirect and direct costs of technology for your organization.

VIGNETTE CHAPTER 2   Out of Funding, Out of Time

Branch School District is a Midwest rural farming community with a population of 74,476. Over the past 10 years, the school district has suffered from hard economic times. This particular case addresses the TCO, which includes internal and external costs, tangible and intangible costs, and long-term costs of technologies. It is also important to consider operational and maintenance costs associated with technologies.

At the superintendent's meeting with the district's school principals, Superintendent Annette Jones Ed. D. announced that the district had received a grant for $1 million for technology purchases. The grant would be divided evenly across the six elementary schools, two middle schools, and two high schools. The purpose of these funds was to increase student reading scores in elementary schools, and to be used in the high schools across the curriculum in learning activities. Principals would ensure the success of every student by ensuring the management of the organization, operation, and resources efficiently using human, fiscal, and technological resources (ELCC 3.0).

Each school received $100,000, and principals decided what they needed in purchases. The principals agreed to work in their respective groups, dividing themselves into an elementary group of six principals, a middle school group of two, and a high school group of two. They planned to keep purchases similar in equipment and software.

The group of elementary principals agreed upon 2 computer labs or centers in each of their buildings. Each lab would contain 30 top-of-the-line computers and software, 2 high-speed printers, 1 Elmo Reader, and 1 ceiling-mounted projector and Smart board. They used the majority of their funding.

The middle school principals decided on 1 computer lab for each school with 30 top-of-the-line computers and software, 2 high-speed printers, 1 Elmo Reader and 1 ceiling-mounted projector and Smart board in each lab. Each school would also receive 2 wireless mobile laptop carts containing 25 computers each, a projector, and a printer. These principals also used the majority of their funding.

The high school principals decided to use their share of the funding to purchase a state-of-the-art distance learning lab with all the bells and whistles. This would increase student engagement and provide many opportunities for students. It would also be used as a staff development center for the entire district and could be used for community education.

At the end of the school year, orders were placed and the equipment arrived during the summer. District computer technicians installed the new equipment, set up the labs with cable and wireless access points, and configured the machines from a program already being used that allows all the computers to have the same software. They set up the projectors and the Smart boards, put together the mobile labs and set up the laptops. Technicians tested the equipment, made necessary configuration changes, and shut the equipment down. They worked throughout the school district, and they finally finished just one week before staff and students returned for the opening of the new school year.

On the first day of school, teachers prepared for their classes and turned on the newly installed computer equipment. The two high schools were first with the wireless laptop carts and the distance learning labs with all the bells and whistles. Next, were the two middle schools with computer labs, and the wireless laptop carts, projectors, Smart boards, and Elmos. Finally, the elementary schools turned on their 360 top-of-the-line computers.

This increase all at one time unexpectedly shut down the main server located at the board of education. There had been a bottleneck in the bandwidth. The Dynamic Host Control Protocol Server "DHCP" shut down as each computer attempted to access network connections for the Internet.

The district computer technicians scrambled to fix the problems, but they didn't understand why they occurred and continued to occur. The superintendent called an emergency meeting of the board of education members who voted on outsourcing the technology problems. After several days of diagnosing, the purchase of several new servers, and a significant increase in bandwidth form the Internet service provider, the entire school district was up and running.

The unexpected tangible cost to the school district was $40,000 for two new servers, a service cost from the outsourced computer company of $10,000, and a monthly district cost for increased bandwidth of $10,000. The total cost to the district budget was reported to be around $170,000.

QUESTIONS

1. Discuss your understanding of the TCO methodologies.

2. Make a list of costs of technology ownership, both direct and indirect.

3. Identify non-operational costs of technology relevant to your organization.

4. Describe the leadership style as it related to the mistake of poor planning.

5. Do you feel that the principals or the superintendent were to blame?

6. Should the superintendent be asked to step down? Why/Why not?

7. What part of the blame should the principals take?

8. If you were a school board member would you call for an investigation?

ACTIVITY

1. In small group discussions identify from the list of stakeholders below the individuals that are affected by the dilemma in the vignette and brainstorm ways they can affect change.

2. How do they communicate and in what forum?

3. Discuss your school or district's written plan of action for this problem, if one exists.

4. Identify any resources that could be utilized to resolve this dilemma.

5. Have one person in your group take notes and share your group's findings in front of the class after the discussion.

6. Organize the consensus.

Outside Government Agencies
Parents
Principals
Staff
Students
Superintendent
Teachers
Technology Personnel

Outside Technology Professionals
Crisis Team
Outside Private Agencies
School Lawyers
Counselor
School Board
Media (TV, Radio, Internet)
State's Attorney

Chapter 3

Acceptable Use Policy

This is the first chapter related to the Risk Assessment Checklist and Profile Instrument. The acceptable use policy will provide the knowledge to help educational leaders identify internal and external cyber threats.

KEY CONCEPTS
Growing technological society
Aspect of enforcing AUPs
Acceptable use policy: legal issues

OBJECTIVES
1. Make a list of acceptable and unacceptable uses of computers and organize them by the components of a policy.
2. Explain why reason and common sense should be the determining factor in considering disciplinary actions for violations of the acceptable use policy.
3. Evaluate an acceptable use policy and describe the strengths and weaknesses of the policy.
4. List five legal reasons why acceptable use policies should be reviewed by an attorney.
5. Explain who the acceptable use policy protects and why.

RELATED ELCC STANDARDS
Standard 1.0
Standard 2.0
Standard 3.0
Standard 4.0
Standard 5.0

INTRODUCTION

In today's growing technological society, it is becoming increasingly important for school districts to protect themselves legally. Legal protection usually comes in the form of acceptable use policies (AUPs). For school leaders establishing these policies has helped shape the way technology is used. AUPs are written agreements signed by users that state specific rules and regulations for technology use. Such policies also outline possible punishments and penalties that can occur if the technology is used inappropriately (iSAFE, 2011). AUPs can be either narrow policies that only address one mode of technology, such as the Internet, or they can be broad policies that encompass all technology used by an organization.

Even though school employees are expected to work only on school-related materials during regular working hours, they may stray into personal email accounts, personal banking, dating sites, music sites, video streaming sites, social networks, and other unrelated school district sites that could have the potential to disrupt the network. This puts both the school and individuals at risk. To make students and employees aware of acceptable computer usages during working and instructional hours, schools need to put AUPs in place.

Every employee and student should review and sign an organizational AUP each year. The policy is a set of rules governing the usage of computers and related technologies. It is vital to the security of the organization that these rules are adhered to for the protection of organizational data as well as the electronic system. These documents should be collected and filed in the respective employee or student folder as a record of understanding.

A general introduction explaining the purpose of school district technology and computer usage for students, teachers, and staff should begin such a policy statement. Next, there should be a brief statement describing acceptable use of school district networks, computers, and other related electronic equipment. The next section should be related to unacceptable usages.

The following document is an example of an AUP designed for a specific school district and has been reviewed by several attorneys. It was adopted by Dorchester County Public School system in Maryland.

THE BOARD OF EDUCATION
ACCEPTABLE USE OF ELECTRONIC EQUIPMENT,
FACILITIES, SERVICES, AND INTERNET SAFETY POLICY

Introduction

It is the general policy of _____ Public Schools that computer systems and network services are to be used as any other instructional medium.

Standards of conduct and use appropriate to an instructional setting are expected of all users. Therefore, computer systems and network services are to be used in a responsible, efficient, ethical, and legal manner in accordance with the mission of the _____ Public Schools. Users of any Schools' computer system or network must acknowledge their understanding of the general policy and guidelines as a condition of use. Use of Schools' computer systems and networks is a privilege, not a right. Failure to adhere to this policy and administrative procedures may result in suspension or revocation of system or network access. Willful or intentional misuse could lead to disciplinary action or criminal penalties under applicable state and federal law.
Provisions:

1. Acceptable uses of _____ Public Schools' systems or networks are activities, which support learning and teaching. System or network users are encouraged to develop uses which meet their individual educational needs and which take advantage of the system or network's functions.

2. Unacceptable uses of _____ Public Schools' systems or networks include, but are not limited to:
   a. Violating the rights to privacy of students or employees of _____ Public Schools, or others outside the school system.
   b. Using profanity, obscenity, or other language, which may be offensive to another user.
   c. Violating United States copyright law.
   d. Plagiarizing is the taking of someone else's words, ideas, or findings and intentionally presenting them as one's own without properly giving credit to their source.
   e. Using the system or network for personal financial gain or for any non-school commercial or any illegal activity.
   f. Attempting to degrade or disrupt system or network performance or unauthorized entry to and/or destruction of computer systems and files.
   g. Re-posting personal email communications without the author's prior consent.
   h. Revealing home phone numbers, addresses, or other personal information.
   i. Making personal purchases or unauthorized orders using the _____ Board of Education name.
   j. Accessing, downloading, storing, or printing files or messages that are sexually explicit, obscene, or which offend or tend to degrade others. The administration invokes its discretionary rights to determine such suitability.

    k. Accessing, downloading, storing, or printing files or messages related to illegal activities, substances, and/or devices which are not permitted by law or by _____ Board of Education Policy and Procedures.

3. Downloading or copying information on to disks or hard drives without prior teacher approval.

4. The staff of _____ Public Schools will be responsible for:
    a. Teaching students the _____ Public Schools Policy and Procedures for system and network services.
    b. Supervising and guiding student access to system and network services to ensure that each student adheres to the appropriate use guidelines.
    c. Installing and monitoring "technology protection measures" that block or filter Internet access to inappropriate sites which are obscene, contain pornography, or are harmful to minors.

5. The following people are entitled to use the network:
    a. All _____ Public School staff and other employees as directed by appropriate authority.
    b. All _____ Public School students under the supervision of a staff member and/or parent/guardian.
    c. Others who request Guest Accounts from the network or system administrator. These requests will be reviewed on a case-by-case basis and will be granted, if warranted, as needs and resources permit.

6. _____ Public Schools makes no express or implied warranties for the Internet access it provides. _____ Public Schools cannot completely eliminate access to information that is offensive or illegal and residing on networks outside of the _____ Schools system. The accuracy and quality of information obtained cannot be guaranteed. _____ Public Schools will not guarantee the availability of access to the Internet and will not be responsible for any information that may be lost, damaged, or unavailable due to technical or other difficulties. Information sent or received cannot be assured to be private.

7. _____ Implementation of the Acceptable Use Policy guarantees Installation of Surf Control across the entire network. Each Internet request is checked against Surf's Control list of acceptable and unacceptable sites as well as personalized lists to ensure that students as well as staff are not able to access inappropriate sites. This filtering tool is

21

active 100 percent of the time on all school computers that are used by students as well as staff.

By signing and dating this document, I _____ (print name) _____ understand and will adhere as a condition of employment, to all the conditions under this policy.

Sign: _____ Date: _____

GROWING TECHNOLOGICAL SOCIETY

Based on experience, after students and staff are reminded of the consequences related to unacceptable use infractions some will test the limits. During 2005, we were briefly involved in a school district-wide audit where our objective was to apply best practices. The purpose of the audit was to determine the amount of time selected teachers and administrators accessed websites that were unrelated to the regular school day. It was an easy audit by tracking (Internet Protocol) IP transmissions of selected logged-on computers. The results of the audit were that 40 percent of the 6.5 hour day the selected teachers and administrators were on sites unrelated to the organization's business. These sites included real estate sites, dating sites, social networks, shopping sites, music sites, and, in one case, porn sites. We would recommend all school districts to conduct an audit of this nature. How could this be happening with filters and border manager software to prevent access?

Filters are software programs that filter out unwanted programs and access to your network. Filters only protect within prescribed parameters, and the filters in the school had not been updated or maintained regularly. Additionally, several teachers used proxy sites to redirect their transmissions, which avoided the filters and border manager software. A proxy site acts as if someone tapped the filter on the shoulder, and when the filter turned to see the transmission; the user went the other way by sneaking around the filter undetected. Proxy sites are often used by students and can remain undetected by filters and border managers.

No matter the scope of the AUP, three common goals are normally addressed. The first goal must be to educate. It is important for not only the organization implementing the AUP to punish those neglecting the rules, but to inform and instruct users (students, staff, and faculty) about why the banned activities are inappropriate for use. The second goal of an AUP is to provide legal notices through which violators can be punished. These legal notices should include, but not be limited to, copyright laws, privacy and ownership laws, and misuse of data and software policies. The third goal of an AUP is to protect the organization from lawsuits. An AUP can protect the organization by making all legal aspects known to both the organization and the user (Standler, 2002). In a perfect world, AUPs and their goals would not be needed; however, today's world and society are not perfect.

Technology also has a dangerous side. Technology users are open to harassment, bullying, identity theft, and hazardous materials such as pornography and hate literature. While these materials can be eliminated through protection software, this software is not concrete and not all hazardous materials can be blocked. Successful blocking is the responsibility of the user, the ultimate filter. AUPs can make the user accountable for his/her actions (iSAFE, 2011). Not only can AUPs protect the user, but also protect the technology as well. Many websites associated with misuse are contaminated and carry multiple viruses. By preventing access and making users accountable for their actions it can reduce the risk of contamination.

Since AUPs vary among the different demographics that they serve, the language used must be at the level of the target population. For example, an AUP used at the high school level would not be appropriate for the elementary school level due to the language and vocabulary. AUPs can also vary depending on the mode of technology. For example, an organization might have separate AUPs for hardware, software, and the Internet. Two main components are needed no matter the age level and mode of technology. First is an explanation of who may access the technology and how information and data is transmitted. Second, an AUP should address which technology is permissible in the organization. This covers both personal and school-based technology. Under these main components are other aspects that need to be incorporated in an AUP. One of these aspects is the philosophies and strategies of the institution involved. Media Awareness (2011) lists the following as important components of an AUP.

- An explanation of the availability of computer networks to students and staff members in the school or district
- A statement about the educational uses and advantages of the Internet
- An explanation of the responsibilities of educators and parents for students' use of the Internet
- A code of conduct governing behaviors on the Internet
- An outline of the consequences of violating the AUP
- A description of what constitutes acceptable and unacceptable use of the Internet
- A description of the rights of individuals using the networks in the school/district (such as the right to free speech, right to privacy, etc.)

23

- A disclaimer absolving the school district from responsibility, under certain circumstances
- An acknowledgement that the AUP complies with provincial and national telecommunication rules and regulations.

(p. 1)

ASPECT OF ENFORCING AUPS

One of the most important features of an AUP is the signature portion. Persons requesting use of technology must sign the policy. This statement discloses the user's intent to follow the rules of use (VDOE, 2011). This feature is only as good as the records kept and the follow-through of the policies and procedures to users. In addition to these components, an important part of an AUP is the disclaimer releasing the school from user wrongdoing (Media Awareness, 2011). All of these components make an AUP a legally binding document, especially if the document is certified by an attorney (Media Awareness, 2011).

Enforcing an AUP can be difficult, but school districts can do this effectively if they incorporate software that can generate data use. For example, software such as eSNIF and VIEW alerts technology administrators when technology is being used inappropriately. These programs not only detect when misuse occurs, but also keep a log of when the misuse occurs and the location of the misuse (Fitzer, 2002). Software can help administrators generate and keep quantitative data on individuals who violate the AUP. No matter the data generator, it is important that the information generated is in a format that can be understood by individuals not fluent in technology.

Another important aspect of enforcing AUPs is to regulate and monitor not only computers, but also personal devices such as laptops, personal digital assistants (PDAs), and other devices (Lightspeed Systems, 2010). This aspect of the educational environment is rapidly expanding. More and more individuals are using personal devices in the classroom, and they can cause problems. Personal devices can cause disruptions in the classroom and are difficult to regulate by the school; however, a highly developed AUP can address these personal devices and can remedy the associated problems. If students and teachers are allowed to bring and use personal devices in schools, that usage must be addressed and monitored by the school district's AUP. Preserving reports and analyzing data are also extremely important in AUP enforcement. Keeping and analyzing reports can depict trends and inappropriate content before it becomes a problem (Lightspeed Systems, 2010). All of these aspects must be addressed in a well-developed AUP.

Discussion, reason, and common sense should be the determining factors in considering disciplinary actions for violations of the AUP. There are many reasons a person could be using technology for the wrong reasons. Disciplinary action should consider the intent of the violator, and the impact of the violation on the individual, constituents, and the organization.

Many school districts use a prescribed template and a series of guidelines that outline the format of the AUP document. These guidelines ensure that all the basic components are incorporated. One such template was compiled by Wentzell (2001). Wentzell advocated that every AUP should have a strong introduction that not only defines what an AUP is, but also the philosophies, educational goals, advantages and disadvantages of technology, and a statement explaining that technology use is a privilege and not a right. Further, Wentzell identified that every strong AUP should have a definitions and vocabulary section to clarify the terms used so all readers understand the context in which the terms are subsequently used.

The next section contained in a successful AUP is the policy section. In this section, specific directives should be given on who, what, where, when, why, and how technology access can be obtained. In the policy section, a statement of privacy needs to be included. This statement of privacy needs to address how privacy is protected and on what grounds. The next section(s) detailed by Wentzell are the copyright and netiquette sections. These sections should explain what copyright laws and netiquette are and specific violations. Personal responsibility is a main component of Wentzell's guidelines. In this section, emphasis is placed on the user and the user's role in technology use. The personal responsibility section works in conjunction with the disclaimer section. Both of these sections take liability from the organization and place it on the user. This is an important section because of the potential for lawsuits. In addition to this is the signature portion and acceptance of the agreement. As stated before, this is most likely the most important portion of the document since it verifies that the user has read and has agreed to the content of the document. This aspect solidifies that the document is a contract and can be used in a court of law. Once this is complete, it should be reviewed and verified by an attorney.

ACCEPTABLE USE POLICY: LEGAL ISSUES

AUPs are probably one of the most used legal contracts in education. AUPs are designed to outline appropriate behaviors and uses of technology and are developed to not only protect the educational system from misuse, but also the user. AUPs are documents developed by an institution and are signed by users. This is a legal and binding contract between the two entities. In the contract, the organization agrees to allow the user to use the equipment mentioned in the document. By signing the document, the user agrees to use the equipment appropriately and in accordance with the policies outlined. Since an AUP is a legal contract, it is important for an attorney to proof the document prior to administration in case the document comes under scrutiny in a court of law. Such documents are part of not only the financial burden faced by the organization, but also the personal burden faced by the user. This personal burden is the dilution of personal freedoms as granted by the U.S. Constitution.

According to the U.S. Constitution, every U.S. citizen is granted the freedoms of speech and expression, privacy, and equal protection under the law. The First Amendment states:

> Congress shall make no law respecting an establishment of religion, or prohibiting the free exercise thereof; or abridging the freedom of speech, or of the press; or the right of the people peaceably to assemble, and to petition the government for a redress of grievances. (U.S. Constitution, Amend. I)

and is a cornerstone of the U.S. lifestyle. This personal freedom is also becoming ever easier to express through the implementation of technology. For example, teachers can incorporate blog sites, email, and social networking sites into courses to create an environment where students can freely communicate with them. These modes of technology can be extremely effective as an educational tool, and according to a literal translation of the U.S. Bill of Rights, are completely permissible. Users are further protected by the U.S. Bill of Rights and the Constitution through the Fourth and Fourteenth Amendments.

The Fourth Amendment protects citizens from illegal searches and seizures, thus strengthening the right to privacy. This can encompass not only a citizen's personal belongings, but also their personal information and communications (U.S. Constitution, Amend. IV). Like the First Amendment, the Fourth Amendment can protect employee email, web sites, and private correspondences. In addition, to the First and Fourth Amendments, employees/users are also protected by the Fourteenth Amendment. The Fourteenth Amendment provides "to any person within its jurisdiction the equal protection of the laws" (U.S. Constitution., Amend. XIV). The Fourteenth Amendment means that all users have to be treated equally and all policies should apply to everyone. The rights of the user should be taken into consideration when developing an AUP because the rights of the user often conflict with the rights and responsibilities of the organization.

Educational institutions have the right to protect not only the technological equipment, but also their integrity and security. To do this, school districts need to develop clear and precise AUPs that outline their needs and what is permitted/ not permitted. A problem occurs when the desires of the users and needs of the institutions conflict. When these conflicts arise, the two parties often dispute these issues in a court of law. Some of these cases eventually arrive at the U.S. Supreme Court.

One such case was the *O'Connor v. Ortega* court case of 1987. In this case, a doctor was charged with sexual harassment of a female subordinate. The doctor was placed on leave to allow the hospital to gather evidence. During the collection of evidence, many of the doctor's personal effects were seized and processed. The doctor sued the hospital on the grounds that the hospital did not have a search warrant and the hospital therefore violated his Fourth Amendment right of no unreasonable searches and seizure. After a long debate, the U.S. Supreme Court decided that "the operational realities of the workplace may make some public employee's expectation of privacy unreasonable" (Findlaw, 2011). This case applies to both education and technology because educators and members of many other organizations are deemed public servants, and they work for the community. Further, while this case dealt with traditional files, it could be expanded to electronic documents such as email and other modes of mass communications. This ruling will be applied in other cases. Employers need only a reasonable suspicion to review employee files (Smith, Woodsum, & MacMahon, 1999). Issues of privacy are not the only facet of debate, First Amendment protections are also debated between users and organizations.

One such case where the First Amendment was debated, *Reno v. ACLU*, established that the Internet is viewed as a public forum and thus is a protected form of speech by the First Amendment. This case also posed the question about whether or not school districts can restrict teacher access to this public forum and what restrictions can be placed on user's First Amendment rights. It has been ruled that organizations, especially school districts, can restrict the First Amendment rights of both students and staff if that form of expression has the reasonable risk of disruption.

This principle, as established by the case *Tinker v. Des Moines*, set a precedent that was later applied to the public forum of the Internet (Tedford & Herbeck, 2006). Additional court cases have also limited the First Amendment rights of staff with technology. This was the case in *Urofsky v. Gilmore* where college professors were accused of accessing explicit materials on computers and equipment owned by the university. The defendants, the professors accused of the actions, were advocating that the suppression of their First Amendment rights were unconstitutional. However, the plaintiffs, the university, took the view point that the computers the employees were using were purchased and owned by the university, and, thus, everything produced on those machines became university property. The court sided with the plaintiffs and determined that, as with all other university property, the computers were under the jurisdiction and control of the university and illegal actions under the university's policy (Smith, Woodsum, & MacMahon, 1999).

In each of the cases mentioned, each institute was protected by a clear and consistent AUP. Further, in each of these cases, there was a concern for the well-being of the organization or privacy of children. Also, in each of these cases the equal protection clause of the Fourteenth Amendment was applied as well as the due process clause. Each of these cases, as well as the AUPs in question, was applied equally to the organization. In most of these matters, the organization wins the debate and the clash between personal freedoms and acceptable use is justified. The organization wins because of the legal aspects of an AUP. These legal aspects are why an attorney must oversee the AUP process. Attorneys not only have a legal grasp of the local environment, but also of the federal environment. Federal law trumps local and state regulations as well as personal freedoms. These federal mandates need to be addressed in AUPs because most people are unfamiliar with such mandates. One example includes the federal Computer Fraud and Abuse Act (CFAA). The CFAA criminalizes any and all computer use "without authorization" (Meyer & Johnson, 2011). This is a broad topic and needs to be addressed specifically for both users and employers so wrongful misuse is not prosecuted in the courts.

CONCLUSION

In summation, an AUP is a series of guidelines that keep both the user and the organization informed about expectations and what actions are acceptable and what are not. This document not only protects the safety of the organization, but also the user. Technology is changing day-to-day interactions, and protection clauses need to be put into place so that all parties involved are protected. Since these protection clauses often conflict with personal rights and responsibilities, it is becoming increasingly important that these clauses be written and certified by an attorney. It is also important to involve an attorney due to the fact that AUPs are contracts, and, like all contracts, can be legally binding and can come under scrutiny, especially when they conflict with personal freedoms.

In Chapters 4–11 you will gain a comprehensive understanding into the supporting related policies behind the acceptable use policy.

QUESTIONS

1. What is acceptable use of technology?

2. What is unacceptable use of technology?

3. Why should an organization have an attorney review the AUP?

4. Who does the AUP protect?

VIGNETTE CHAPTER 3 Pause

Ms. Araya is the principal of PS 132, a large inner-city school with over 800 students. She is respected by colleagues and community members as a fair and ethical leader. Ms. Araya has the full support of her staff and faculty and has managed to create a positive culture of learning. Mr. Chin, the district supervisor, recently contacted Ms. Araya by phone to report that one of her teachers had been viewing pornography on a school computer.

Mr. Chin shared that he received information from the central office network administrator which included a computer printout of several occasions that the teacher had acquired photos of persons engaged in sexual activities. The IP (Internet Protocol) address of the computer and the logon access and password coincided with the teacher's computer being logged on to the network and in use during these incidents. Ms. Araya and Mr. Chin immediately met to discuss the investigation.

As Mr. Chin provided evidence gathered over the past two weeks, Ms. Araya's reaction was bland. According to his information, the teacher accessed pornography six times in the morning just before the school day started. Ms. Araya acted prudently and called the teacher to her office in the presence of Mr. Chin. She also requested that a representative from the Teacher Union be present during the meeting.

Ms. Adams was the 26-year-old teacher at the center of the investigation. She and the union representative were presented with the computer records and evidence, and they were given time to review and discuss the information. Ms. Araya asked Ms. Adams to explain the material on the computer in her classroom. Ms. Adams explained that she did not know how the material got there and said it was "just there." Mr. Chin showed Ms. Adams a signed copy of the district's strictly-enforced AUP signed by her at the start of the school year. He pointed out the sub-section on possession of explicit material. Following district policy, Ms. Adams was immediately suspended by Ms. Araya and escorted off school property pending a hearing.

After the suspension, Mr. Chin explained that the evidence was cut and dry. He believed that Ms. Adams would most likely resign instead of being embarrassed with a hearing. Ms. Araya asked Mr. Chin to pause and reexamine the evidence. She shared that she knew Ms. Adams well and respected her work as a teacher in the school. Mr. Chin reminded Ms. Araya of the district's strict policies and her good reputation as principal of PS 132. He asked her if she truly wanted to pause and reinvestigate this infraction. Ms. Araya responded by saying that she wanted to question the network administrator.

Several days later, Ms. Araya met with the network administrator and inquired about the behavior and intent of the accused teacher. The network administrator explained that the data showed the teacher's computer under her logon was identified as downloading explicit material from a web site. Ms. Araya asked if the teacher's intent could be determined at the time of the download. The network administrator only reiterated his prior response.

Ms. Araya still had unanswered questions, so she sought advice from her former university technology professor. After viewing the evidence, the professor showed Ms. Araya how the pornography was accessed on Ms. Adams computer. The explicit materials came into Ms. Adam's classroom computer as a download attachment through her personal email account. It was detected by the central office network administrator through an alert or during an audit when it downloaded.

The current AUP did not address access to personal email accounts while using district electronic equipment. Ms. Adams was reinstated the next day.

QUESTIONS

1. Did Ms. Araya promote a culture of continual and sustainable improvement?

2. Did the network administrator act with prudence?

3. Did Mr. Chin act with prudence?

4. What were the miscommunications between Ms. Araya and the network administrator?

5. Did Ms. Adams have grounds for a lawsuit if she was terminated?

6. What recommendations would you have for the board of education and the superintendent?

7. Did Ms. Araya support developing and supervising the instructional and leadership capacity and promote the most effective and appropriate technologies to support teaching and learning?

8. Did Ms. Araya act with integrity, fairness, and in an ethical manner to ensure a system of accountability? How?

9. In reference to the allegations posed at the beginning of the vignette, who was at fault for the existence of pornographic materials in the school and why?

ACTIVITY

1. In small group discussions identify from the list of stakeholders below the individuals that are affected by the dilemma in the vignette and brainstorm ways they can affect change.

2. How do they communicate and in what forum?

3. Discuss your school or district's written plan of action for this problem, if one exists.

4. Identify any resources that could be utilized to resolve this dilemma.

5. Have one person in your group take notes and share your group's findings in front of the class after the discussion.

6. Organize the consensus.

Outside Government Agencies	Outside Technology Professionals
Parents	Crisis Team
Principals	Outside Private Agencies
Staff	School Lawyers
Students	Counselor
Superintendent	School Board
Teachers	Media (TV, Radio, Internet)
Technology Personnel	State's Attorney

Chapter 4

Authentication Policy

The authentication policy is another aspect of the Risk Assessment Checklist and Profile Instrument. This will provide educational leaders the knowledge to understand authorization, identification, and authentication.

KEY CONCEPTS
Authentication policy
Password authentication
System-specific authentication

OBJECTIVES
1. Define secure socket layers, ciphers and encryption in an authentication policy.
2. Identify and describe the intrusions and threats which an authentication policy protects a system from.
3. Discuss what the organization considers an asset and why.

RELATED ELCC STANDARDS
Standard 3.0
Standard 5.0

INTRODUCTION

The use of authorization, identification, and authentication control ensures that only known users make use of information systems. The California Technology Assistance Project (CTAP) that supports California K-12 educational technologies states: "Without authorization, identification, and authentication controls, information systems could be accessed illicitly and that the security of those information systems could be compromised" (Authorization, Identification, and

Authentication Policy Template, 2011). School leaders must understand the authentication policy is to ensure that only authorized users have access to specific computers. Security requirements are made for setting up user accounts, enabling user access, and ensuring the user is properly authenticated at a particular site (Kobus, 2007). The authentication policy is also used to mitigate the risk of unauthorized access of information, establish user accountability, and establish rules for access. This policy is a key aspect of trust-based identity attribution providing a codified assurance of the identity of one entity to another. The authentication policy controls who is allowed to use the equipment and who is not.

AUTHENTICATION TOOLS AND DEVICES

The authentication policy can be performed by using various tools, devices, network equipment, and through the use of different protocols. The ability to identify a user during a web transaction is crucial to isolate threats and enable policy enforcement with a specific behavior for each user or group (User Identification & Authentication, 2007). The option to identify or authenticate the user is dependent on the network layout and the security rules that are used (User Identification & Authentication, 2007). No single solution applies to all organizations; therefore, a solution should be flexible and feasible enough to offer support for multiple technology systems. Authentication devices can be used to isolate the network and perform direct access to an authentication server from a secured zone.

The policy permits access to the various organizations' information assets. Each information asset is granted on different levels. The different levels are based on the business rules established by the owner or an authorized user. This enables the system entity to create, read, update, delete, or transmit specific information (Kobus, 2007). The organization only allows access to certain users based on privileged information. Most organizations require that systems be protected from unauthorized access by establishing requirements for the authorization and management of user accounts, providing user authentication, and implementing access controls (Kobus, 2007). This information will be managed and controlled through discretion access controls, identification and authentication, and audit trails (Kobus, 2007).

Many educational sites and health organizations have their employees' and customers' confidential information on file within their system. Every effort is made to avoid outside parties gaining access or breaching security; otherwise, any known or unknown information exploited is perceived as a security incident. Once confidential information is released, the organization handles the situation in accordance with established incident reporting guidelines and appropriate human resource policies and procedures (Kobus, 2007). There are several methods for authenticating users. If an authentication method is selected, the system will not run until the users are authenticated.

PASSWORD AUTHENTICATION

If the user selects password authentication, each must set a password the first time the system runs and enter that password each time the system runs thereafter (Vmware, 2011). Password authentication may be appropriate in various circumstances, especially if end users need to run their system when they are not connected to the organization's network. If end users forget their password, they can create a request to the system that sends them to a designated administrator (Vmware, 2011). The administrator can reset the password and provide a new password to the end user. The end-user enters the new password to run the system and sets a new password (Vmware, 2011).

InfoTech Research Group stated "the provision of this confidential information includes a username, a complex password, an answer to a pre-arranged security question, and the confirmation of the owner's email address . . . normally, this process is used when enrolling online to personal accounts, to prevent another user from gaining personal information" (Authorization, Identification, and Authentication Policy Template, 2011). The use of the organization's information assets shall be restricted, and shall be provided only to necessary authorized personnel. The organization's user-based access controls shall be reviewed for sufficient security-level access and protection frequently and consistently. If the organization finds a problem with the security and protection of confidential information, the user would be notified and precaution measures would be taken. To ensure the security and integrity of both organizational data and data belonging to individuals, all organizational owners of computer systems and networks must develop and implement access control policies. Authentication is the secure identification of system users. The system administrator is responsible for determining which authentication method to use among those that may be available for a particular system.

This setting is appropriate only if the technology system has no access to sensitive information and can be made widely available. For example, this setting might be appropriate for distributing demonstrations without restrictions. Some organizations email their employees with memos, spreadsheets, or files to view. This type of demonstration would be sent via email to all employees without restrictions. Identifiers are the key used by organizations for identification relationships. Identifiers may be classified as omni-directional or omni–uni-directional. Omni-directional identifiers are intended to be public and easily discoverable. Omni–uni-directional identifiers are intended to be private and used only in the context of a specific identity relationship.

SYSTEM-SPECIFIC AUTHENTICATION

All organizational information is considered an asset and is protected by security. However, "system owners are strongly encouraged to rely on the authentication services provided by the organization they are with rather than using system-specific authentication methods" (InfoTech, 2011). This service provides secure authentication and consistent identification. This policy applies to all aspects of qualifying transactions, including initiation, routing, and processing. Secure identification of the participants in all such transactions is crucial to the successful conduct of the organization. Security protocols for these businesses and organizations call for the distribution of confidentiality forms, integrity forms, and availability forms to their employees and customers (Kobus, 2007). Identifiers may also be classified as resolvable or non-resolvable. Resolvable identifiers are domain names or email addresses. Non-resolvable identifiers are a person's real world name or a topic name.

User identification is required for authorization, policy enforcement, auditing, identification, and authentication. The authorization is used to identify whether the specified user is authorized to use the system or apart from the specific organization. The policy is enforced by applying the right policy to the user. Auditing is used to trace the activity of the user in recording detailed transactions for future viewing and analysis of activities performed by the user (User Identification and Authentication, 2007). This prevents users from accessing websites that are job-related, or related to that organization.

In some cases the authentication causes a pop-up window to appear to make sure that the end-user is legitimate, and sometimes a site key is required as identified by the user. The identification at this point can identify the user based on the source IP address or identify the user according to credentials by challenging the user to send the credentials. If the user is already authenticated in the network, the end-user's browser will automatically send the required credentials to the system. The authentication is used when the user/domain information is obtained and validated. In cases where real-user authentication is required, the authentication is performed through the use of an authentication service. A dedicated authentication device has three main benefits: performance, security, and high availability (User Identification and Authentication, 2007).

CONCLUSION

Policy implementation should be based upon the use of management-approved security standards, procedures, and organizational best practices. Newly developed applications should follow specific standards appropriately. Any existing applications can be assessed to determine feasibility of migration to standards as enhancements or upgrades. Other systems and applications should follow other requirements.

QUESTIONS

1. Describe the purpose of authorization, identification, and authentication.

2. What does authorization, identification, and authentication protect an organization from?

3. What is the organization protecting? Why?

VIGNETTE CHAPTER 4   Another Way Around

Mr. Evans is a 20-year principal of North Woods Senior High School located in an east coast urban community. He is known for his high visibility among the faculty and students and does routine unscheduled classroom walk-through visits.

During his routine classroom walk through, Principal Evans noticed that many students were not engaged in learning because they were on social network sites. Mr. Evans raised his concerns at the next faculty meeting. Because he is a participative leader, he was open to suggestions from his staff. At the meeting, Mr. Evans reviewed the policy with the teachers. It addressed iPods, cell phones, and other electronic devices banned for use by students during school hours.

The consensus among the staff members was to have the district's network administrator block social network sites from the server. As a result, social network sites would not be allowed to be displayed on any school computers. Mr. Evans contacted the network administrator who agreed to block all social networking sites from entering the district's network. For the next two weeks, Mr. Evans did not see any students on social network sites and learning progressed.

Several weeks later, Mr. Evans again observed students on social network sites. In fact they were the same sites that he believed had been blocked. He contacted the network administrator who said that was impossible. He even checked the list of blocked sites in the district network management software, and they were reported blocked.

Mr. Evans called an unscheduled afternoon staff meeting and shared this information with his faculty. He asked them again for insights and suggestions into this dilemma. Ms. Jones, a teacher who had a child at the school, said she would ask her son if he knew anything about the situation. Her son explained that they were all using a proxy site to get past the blocked sites. The child explained that these sites allow the social network site to get through by redirecting the transmission.

Ms. Jones shared what she learned from her son with Mr. Evans the next day. Mr. Evans addressed the students during morning announcements. He explained that the use of social network sites would be banned at the school, even though they were not specifically addressed in the signed Acceptable Use Policy. He did not let on that he knew about the proxy sites being used. Mr. Evans did announce that any students found to be on a social network site would be in violation of his new policy and would be subject to disciplinary action or even suspension. He said a letter would be going home with the students at the end of the day notifying their parents of the new policy. The letter was to be signed and returned. Without the signed and returned letter, students would not be allowed to use school computers.

Mr. Evans notified the superintendent of schools of his actions and decisions. In a memo, he explained to the superintendent that social networks are blocked at school, but with the simple use of a proxy the blocked site can be redirected to the student's computer. Mr. Evans shared there are even encryption proxy sites to get past complex encryption and secure socket layers (SSL). They can be bi-directional or uni-directional regenerating encryption keys. Even if you block proxy sites, students would be able to access proxy sites in other languages.

Mr. Evans contacted the local wireless company where some of his past students were employed. They were more than willing to help out their old principal. Mr. Evans had to suspend several students over the next couple of weeks, but the use of proxy sites eventually stopped.

QUESTIONS

1. If you were Mr. Evans, what recommendations would you have made to the superintendent and the board of education?

2. Would you have acted in the same manner as Mr. Evans with the faculty?

3. Did the students who were caught on the proxy sites after the letters were returned deserve to be suspended?

4. What recommendations would you make to the network administrator?

5. Should the network administrator have simply blocked the Internet proxy sites as well? Explain.

6. Would you have contacted anyone else at the central office?

ACTIVITY

1. In small group discussions identify from the list of stakeholders below the individuals that are affected by the dilemma in the vignette and brainstorm ways they can affect change.

2. How do they communicate and in what forum?

3. Discuss your school or district's written plan of action for this problem, if one exists.

4. Identify any resources that could be utilized to resolve this dilemma.

5. Have one person in your group take notes and share your group's findings in front of the class after the discussion.

6. Organize the consensus.

Outside Government Agencies	Outside Technology Professionals
Parents	Crisis Team
Principals	Outside Private Agencies
Staff	School Lawyers
Students	Counselor
Superintendent	School Board
Teachers	Media (TV, Radio, Internet)
Technology Personnel	State's Attorney

Chapter 5

Internet-Use Policy

Internet-use policy is addressed in the Risk Assessment Checklist and Profile Instrument. This chapter will assist educational leaders in understanding appropriate use of equipment and the cyber culture of their organization.

KEY CONCEPTS
Internet-use policies utilizing filters
Downloading policy
Explicit materials rule
Video and media streaming rule (including music, games, dating rules)
Pop-ups and advertising rule
Email rules
Other organizational rules

OBJECTIVES
1. List and explain many different methods used to block Internet sites.
2. Explain the term "user blocking."
3. Compare how the Internet-use policy and the acceptable use policy are related. How do they differ?
4. Describe the different forms of media streaming.
5. Create a list of downloadable materials and explain how each of these could affect operations.
6. Relate other organizational rules to the download policy.

RELATED ELCC STANDARDS
Standard 1.0
Standard 3.0
Standard 5.0
Standard 6.0

INTRODUCTION

The increased use of the Internet at work has forced school district officials to implement an Internet use policy. Internet-use policy, also known as an IUP, and addressed in Chapter 3, is a legal document designed to inform employees of appropriate use and professional conduct while using an Internet system.

School leaders must understand that complex components in the Internet use policy determine its impact on the culture of an organization. These components include downloading, utilizing filters, video streaming, pop-ups, advertising rules, email usage, and other organizational rules. The Internet use policy is designed to make distinctions between work uses and discourage personal use in a professional working environment (Arnesen & Weis, 2007). The Internet use policy is part of the AUP and is supported within the acceptable use signed legal document. This policy governs monitors and restricts the use of assigned electronic equipment through the use of filters.

With the advent of peer-2-peer systems, iTunes, and other sites that allow the downloading of software and materials, it is becoming important for institutions to restrict user access. The restriction of downloading is not only a way to protect the institution, but also the employees. This is why many institutions are developing strict policies about downloading dangers to prevent misuse. It is the responsibility of the educational leader to be aware of the organizational rules as they relate to the download policy and to routinely update this policy. A policy is roughly defined as a document that outlines rules and regulations (SANS, 2011). Policies concerning electronics and computers usually address specific issues and/or are comprised into an IUP. One of the issues is a download policy. In this policy, an organization needs to outline what users can/cannot download on computers owned and operated by the organization. By restricting downloads, an organization can control and prevent security breaches, such as viruses. These viruses can corrupt or transfer data and ultimately make the organization vulnerable to attack. Viruses can be attached to downloadable material and can degrade equipment or send valuable information to hackers. Restricting downloads can also reduce levels of bandwidth and memory space for the organization. Often, when downloading occurs, Internet access becomes slow. This overuse can be costly financially for the organization. It can also wear out the system. The more the bandwidth and computers are used the more it costs in either repair or operating fees. A download policy also addresses issues of copyright infringement and violation. Many of the sites that provide downloads are not authorized to do so, or fail to adhere to federal licensing agreements. This can be troublesome not only for the user, but also the organization. These actions can lead to severe fines and federal copyright violation charges (Norton, 2002). Users many not know about many of these issues, or may not be educated about how to prevent them. This is why many organizations, such as universities and school districts, have specific downloading policies to protect data.

INTERNET-USE POLICIES UTILIZING FILTERS

The technology departments in school districts reserve the right to load filtering software on technology equipment to prohibit access from inappropriate websites. Internet filters are common tools used to limit access to certain materials on the World Wide Web.

Many different methods are used to block Internet sites. Using filtering software is just one method. Keyword blocking is a common approach used by many filtering programs. To eliminate user's efforts from gaining access to a site, technology administrators use a predetermined list of words. Site blocking programs are designed to prevent certain users from gaining access to specific sites on the Internet. Many of the Internet's blocking programs have the capacity to block domain level sites. Protocol blocking prevents access to specific types of Internet services such as Usenet and FTP (File Transfer Protocol) Internet services. Due to the high level of inappropriate sites on the Internet, technology administrators employ protocol blocking to prevent those Internet services from access to the district servers. User blocking is used widely in school districts. Adopting the user blocking system, users are then provided with identification name, pass code, and access code, which determine the level of access. Teachers, students, and administrators are given different levels of access through their identification information. Organizations decide if and how they are going to keep track of the usage of these digital tools (Project, n.d.).

The district and building administrator should have advanced knowledge of the level of access their students, staff, and faculty have to the Internet and World Wide Web. This is typically not spelled out in the AUP, but is generalized, and responsibility to protect the students, staff, and faculty falls upon the district and building administrators. Reasonable or limited protection is not enough today in this environment of cyber threats of intrusions. For example, given the high rate of its technology management turnover, one school district failed to maintain its filters (this is described in full in the chapter's vignette). A media specialist and 2nd grade teacher in this district were teaching the class about the White House, and a porn site called White House accidently projected on the large screen to all the children, which otherwise would have been restricted by the filters. Who is responsible when the news media, PTA, parents, and community church leaders contact you, the administrator? Let's review ELCC standard 3.0 which states:

> An education leader applies knowledge that promotes the success of every student by ensuring the management of the organization, operation, and resources through monitoring and evaluating management and

operational systems; efficiently using human, fiscal, and technological resources; promoting policies and procedures that protect the welfare and safety of students and staff; developing capacity for distributed leadership; and ensuring that time focuses on high-quality instruction and student learning.

Data protection is another real concern of district and building administrators. While the filters and boarder manager software restrict outgoing Internet requests and searches they also restrict incoming transmissions. Filters and border manager software assist and reinforce the services provided by the firewalls. These concepts are discussed in detail in later chapters.

DOWNLOADING POLICY

Downloading is any transfer of data or copying of data from one computer to another, or to a disk or peripheral device, or transferred by any of these methods. The Internet-use policy and filters should allow users to download appropriate instructional material only. The downloading policy is applicable to all users.

EXPLICIT MATERIALS RULE

In the policy statement, users are warned not to use the school district technology resources to access, review, upload, download, store, print, post, or distribute pornographic, obscene, or sexually explicit or suggestive material. This rule is only as good as are the preventive software filters. These filters should be regularly managed with upgrades of definitions.

VIDEO AND MEDIA STREAMING RULE (INCLUDING MUSIC, GAMES, DATING RULES)

Video and/or media streaming data transmitted through computer networks for immediate playback, rather than for file download and later offline playback, is a concern of organizations since it requires use of large amounts of bandwidth. An example of video and audio streaming includes data downloaded from radio and television broadcasts, and other organizations' webcasts. The Internet-use policy and appropriate-use guidelines should clearly define what users can and cannot do regarding video streaming. Filters should be in place to determine and restrict the downloading of streaming media. Network changes can be made by the network administrator restricting such activities. Below are example policy statements:

Policy Statement: Users will not use the District's Technology Resources to gain unauthorized access to information resources or to access other people or organization's material, information, or files without the implied or direct permission of the person. Under personal use und the Internet-use policy: Excessive personal surfing, utilizing streaming services such as listening to music or watching videos, and downloading of music and video files are specially forbidden.

POP-UPS AND ADVERTISING RULE

Three types of pop-ups exist: general browser pop-ups, Messenger Service advisements, and pop-ups generated by Adware and Spyware. Each of these pop-ups can be controlled by installing a pop-up blocker. In many cases, pop-ups in any form will interfere with the ability to see relevant information on the computer monitor. Many of the pop-ups and advertisements can include Malware, Adware, Spyware, or viruses that are designed to destroy and disrupt data and software programs on the computer or server. As part of the Internet-use policy, the Department of Technology should have the resources to purchase anti-virus software packages and aggressively eliminate any virus that may affect the network. Updates should be scheduled and monitored routinely by the network administrator.

EMAIL RULES

The administrator should determine the use of email by way of the Internet. Inappropriate use of email includes, but is not limited to, sending or forwarding any form of written document. As a recommendation, all emails should be restricted to the organization's email system and use of personal email should be restricted and blocked. Network administrators can install filters and restrict the use of outside and personal email transmissions during work hours. These actions will restrict the following actions persons can attach to personal email files:

- Pornographic or sexually explicit materials
- Games or other software or copyrighted materials without a legitimate business or instructional purpose
- Materials related to personal commercial ventures or solicitations for personal gain (for example messages that could be considered pyramid schemes)
- Information related to religious materials, activities or causes, including inspirational messages.

Clearly, there are an increasing number of cases involving abuse of the Internet and email systems. Abuse of the Internet and email also results in significant lost productivity and instructional time (Arnesen & Weis, 2007).

OTHER ORGANIZATIONAL RULES

Employees should be reminded that it is inappropriate to reveal confidential information or any other material covered by the organizational confidentiality policies and procedures on the Internet. Employees releasing such confidential information, whether the release is inadvertent or not, should be subject to the penalties provided by the organization's policies and procedures. Other rules should include hours of user access and operation, which can be set by the network administrator.

For a download policy to be specific it must identify most, if not all, of the types of downloadable material and provide a definition that even the most technologically inexperienced individual could understand. For example, Howard University's download policy addresses specifically MP3s and MP4s and copyright standards. This policy also addresses why illegal downloading can be harmful and the repercussions for violations (Howard University, 2011). This is important because it lessens the likelihood of a person mistakenly violating the policy. Other universities and institutions are also implementing in their policies a system of warnings and punishments for violations. Enforcement for the policy is the key. Elon University has expanded the school's honor code and AUP to include inappropriate and illegal downloads. In addition, Elon University has also mounted detection software and assessed fines in addition to disciplinary actions for violators (Hill, 2011).

These aspects should be applied at any institution or school; however, in most institutions, there is no immediate need for downloads. In these schools, it would be in the best interest to prevent any and all downloads and changes to the system. In such a situation, the only personnel allowed to download and make changes to programs would be those with either the appropriate security clearance or the IT professionals responsible for network maintenance. This practice is the only way to prevent illegal downloading.

CONCLUSION

In conclusion, due to the high level of inappropriate sites on the Internet and the thousands of daily threats, the best practices are to lockdown the network with filters, pass codes, access codes, and any device that limits access to the work-related data system. The downloading practices of users can be a hindrance in efficiency and performance. Downloads corrupt systems and slow down computer performance. Downloads can also take up valuable memory and storage space. This is why school districts need to develop a download policy that can control and protect the data investment. The next chapter examines the access of electronic equipment.

QUESTIONS

1. Are there similarities between AUPs and Internet-use policies? Explain.

2. What outside forces do Internet-use policies protect an organization from?

3. What types of software and hardware is used for Internet-use policies?

4. What is the importance of downloading policies?

5. How does downloading protect the organization/employee/student?

6. How is this policy expressed in the AUP?

VIGNETTE CHAPTER 5   Utilizing Filters

West Long Shore Elementary School in the community of Long Shore is a west coast private school with a population of 1200 students. Located in a wealthy community and surrounded by small estate homes the school is well funded. The headmaster, Mr. Rider, has been principal at West Long Shore Elementary School for 15 years. The teacher Ms. May has been a 1st grade teacher for 32 years and is considering retirement.

Ms. May's 1st grade class was in the computer lab located in the media center, learning more about the White House and United States presidents. She instructed them to use the pull-down browser menu and click on Google. She had them follow her steps as she searched for information on the instructor's computer, which was connected to the projector. Ms. May searched Google Images for "White House", and a porn site appeared showing explicit material. All of the children were shocked. Some laughed, others pointed, and several began to cry. Ms. May became sick to her stomach and clicked out of the site as quickly as possible.

Knowing that these children had been exposed to inappropriate content, she gently explained that this was not what she had planned to show them. Ms. May told the children that there must have been a computer error. She contacted the headmaster, Mr. Rider, who responded to the media center to view the history on the computer.

Mr. Rider called the central office of the private school and gave instructions for a letter to be sent home with the students who were exposed to the images. In the letter, Mr. Rider explained the situation to parents. He also shared that he had computer technicians investigating the incident, and that a counselor would be talking to the children in the morning. When the parents read the letter, several contacted the PTA and the local newspaper reporting that the school showed the 1st grade students a porn site.

The next morning the local news media was waiting for the school to open so they could inquire about the allegations. Mr. Rider had no comment and requested that the media leave the property as they could interfere with school operations. The media questioned parents in the school's parking lot. Several parents shared the letter Mr. Rider sent home and expressed their anger. The PTA and the school's board members contacted Mr. Rider, and he explained to them that the incident was under investigation. He said he could not comment without all the facts.

Later that day the technicians reported their findings to Mr. Rider:

1. The teacher workstation settings in the media center were not locked down, therefore parent control settings could have been changed.
2. The safe searches Google settings were changed as a result of the computer not being locked down, which allowed all materials to stream.
3. The district filters were down because the last technology manager moved and no one was aware of the contract expiring. Therefore, the entire school district was unfiltered.
4. The teacher workstation did not have a clean slate default program, so settings could be changed to access all websites.

The school's central office made it clear to Mr. Rider that the problem needed to be resolved immediately. The pressure was on, and Mr. Rider needed to take quick action to handle the situation and convince others that it wouldn't happen again.

QUESTIONS

1. Should anyone review the policies? Who?

2. Did Mr. Rider cover up the situation or use "need-to-know" comments?

3. Do you feel that the technicians, media specialist, or teacher was at fault? Why/Why not?

4. If you were a parent, would the information you received have been sufficient?

5. Why do you feel the central office acted the way they did?

6. As the building administrator, what would you have done differently?

7. Describe how Mr. Rider promoted policies and procedures that protect the welfare and safety of students and staff.

8. Would a public school respond differently to this problem than a private school?

ACTIVITY

1. In small group discussions identify from the list of stakeholders below the individuals that are affected by the dilemma in the vignette and brainstorm ways they can affect change.

2. How do they communicate and in what forum?

3. Discuss your school or district's written plan of action for this problem, if one exists.

4. Identify any resources that could be utilized to resolve this dilemma.

5. Have one person in your group take notes and share your group's findings in front of the class after the discussion.

6. Organize the consensus.

Outside Government Agencies
Parents
Principals
Staff
Students
Superintendent
Teachers
Technology Personnel

Outside Technology Professionals
Crisis Team
Outside Private Agencies
School Lawyers
Counselor
School Board
Media (TV, Radio, Internet)
State's Attorney

Chapter 6

Access Policy

Access policy is addressed in the Risk Assessment Checklist and Profile Instrument. This chapter provides educational leaders knowledge into appropriate areas of access for computer users.

KEY CONCEPTS
Password and logon requirements and complexities
Monitoring and auditing/network access
Rights and privileges
Unattended idle configuration
Wireless access
Wireless access tools
Remote access
Frozen workstations with Deepfreeze or Clean Slate
Biometrics

OBJECTIVES
1. Describe password complexities.
2. Develop an access policy and explain how it will protect an organization's data.
3. Define and explain how idle configurations are protected by frozen workstations.

RELATED ELCC STANDARDS
Standard 2.0
Standard 3.0
Standard 5.0

INTRODUCTION

Use of computers and access to the Internet are essential tools in the information age. Technology and various software programs can help increase productivity and efficiency in every discipline across the spectrum. Some K-12 organizations have recognized an emerging problem with the way employees are using their computers at work. Educational leaders should stay ahead of these emerging problems. According to Arnesen and Weis (2007), of the employees who access the Internet, more than 60 percent admitted they used the Internet while at work for personal reasons (Websense, 2006). There is a surge of K-12 organizations and companies working to change their culture by promoting appropriate Internet use to eliminate legal liability, security threats, and decreased productivity. Consequently, K-12 organizations are essentially paying employees to use the Internet for personal use, but also increasing personnel and legal liability costs. Arnesen and Weis (2007) restated that other studies showed employees who surfed the Internet accumulated 220 hours per year for non-business use (Carswell, 2001). Organizations can take a proactive approach by implementing Internet-use policies, buying monitoring software, and hiring additional technology personnel to change the digital landscape. The headings below are terms and concepts related to access so educational leaders can gain a greater understanding of them. The chapter also discusses best practice recommendations.

PASSWORD AND LOGON REQUIREMENTS AND COMPLEXITIES

Effective policy statements should address the following:

- All pass codes, passwords, IDs, and encrypted information are the property of the organization.
- No user may use a pass code, password, ID, or method of encryption that has not been issued specifically to that user by the district. In other words, no user may give, even on a temporary basis, his/her code, password, or ID to another user without prior written approval by the district.
- Every user is responsible for, and should take all the reasonable precautions to protect, his/her pass code, password, and ID Passwords are an important aspect of computer security. A poorly chosen password may result in unauthorized access and/or exploitation of the school district. All users, including contractors and vendors with access to school district, are responsible for taking the appropriate steps to secure their password.

MONITORING AND AUDITING/NETWORK ACCESS

Usage of all of a school district's technology resources and any electronic data created, sent, received, or stored in the system are, and remain, the property of the organization. The organization treats all electronic data sent, received, or stored through its technology resources as its business information. As a result, the organization has the right and duty to periodically assess whether their technology resources and all electronic data generated and stored within those resources are the property of the district; users should understand that they have no expectation of privacy.

K-12 administrators should recognize they have a responsibility to know when employees are using the Internet to gamble, download illegal music or movies, use social networks and online dating services during work. The Aberdeem Group, a leading computer industry market research firm, analysis and consulting organization says, "If employees are left unrestricted by policy and unchecked by monitoring software, then the corporation has exposed itself to significant legal liabilities, probable bandwidth abuse, and employee productivity gaps."

RIGHTS AND PRIVILEGES

The use of the district's technology resources is a privilege, not a right, which may be revoked by the district at any time and for any reason. Depending on the nature and the degree of the violation and the number of previous violations of unacceptable use of the district's technology resources, misuse may result in one or more of the following consequences:

- Suspension or cancellation of use or access privileges to the district technology resources
- Facing other disciplinary action in keeping with the disciplinary polices and guidelines
- Civil or criminal liability under other applicable laws.

According to Digital Ethics (2012) there are several laws that regulate employee rights to privacy, but they can be interpreted in different ways and thus are not always clear for interpretation. The Federal Criminal Codes discuss the interception of electronic communication where the line between personal and work property is hazy. The Civil Rights Act protects against employee discrimination, including the use of electronic monitoring. The Fourth Amendment protects U.S. citizens from unreasonable search and seizure, but does not protect workers while at work. Work information is not personal and is not protected under this law. The Electronic Communication Privacy Act of

1986 states that it is a crime to intercept any type of communication willfully, but it adds that it must affect interstate or foreign commerce.

UNATTENDED IDLE CONFIGURATION

When a computer is left unattended and logged onto a network, the user invites unauthorized access, alteration, or deletion of data. Unattended software was created to free technicians from routine work such as tedious and time-consuming program installation, but still keeping the workstations secure. Unattended software programs are designed to be installed on the master personal computer or the network. The unattended software records and downloads programs or updates to the network so the system is functioning properly. Another type of unattended idle configuration relates to unattended computers. Network administrators should set parameters to limit the time a computer can be left on while unattended. This security option will limit the opportunity of those unauthorized persons intending to access the system.

WIRELESS ACCESS

In a computer networking system, a wireless access point (WAD) is a device that allows wireless devices to connect to a wired network using Wi-Fi, Bluetooth, or other related standard wireless equipment. The WAD usually connects with a router (via wired network) and can relay data between the wireless devices (such as computers or printers) and wired devices on the network. The network connection folder and the message displayed in the notification area of the task bar provide information about the state of the wireless network availability as well as authentication and connection status. For best practices no network should be "open" to random access according to wire access tool rules.

WIRELESS ACCESS TOOLS

All wireless networks should be accessible only when prompted by a proper user and password. Wireless "open" network hot spots allow for violations of the AUP. These settings can be utilized and secured by the network administrator.

REMOTE ACCESS

Technology allows the IT professional to perform administrative tasks to run programs on a remote computer as if they were working locally. Access is gained to another computer located anywhere, and from a different terminal, to perform administrative and routine tasks and also in some cases allows employees access. Best practices should only allow remote access with user ID and authentication and password. For added security site keys should be used.

FROZEN WORKSTATIONS WITH DEEPFREEZE OR CLEAN SLATE

Deepfreeze is a kernel level driver that protects hard drive integrity by redirecting information being written to the hard drive or partition while leaving the original data intact. Deepfreeze can also protect a computer from harmful Malware, since it automatically deletes or downloads files when the computer restarts. Clean Slate is designed to reconfigure drivers back to their original state upon rebooting or logging off. The software program restores the computer to its original configuration, discarding unwanted user changes, including erased files, installed software, downloaded Spyware and Adware. This software protection only allows storage on a network fold and will return the computer to a preset default setting. These best practices are vital for computers and systems to remain stable.

BIOMETRICS

Biometrics identification system allows technicians to input a person's contact information, using fingerprint recognition software, to capture a digital photograph, and retrieve his/her fingerprints from a central console. However, most organizations do not use this type of security as it has been found that it can be accessed with ease.

CONCLUSION

The access policy should clearly state the purpose and intent of the school district. The intent of this policy is to inform employees of district expectations so they can govern themselves in a professional manner. The purpose of these policies is to provide support to employees through the use of technology; therefore, anyone who utilizes the Internet or district's technology systems must foster that purpose by using Internet resources only for educational purposes and in an appropriate and legal manner. All employees using the Internet whether from a school or from a remote location or with technology sponsored hardware, software, and/or accounts should be prohibited from using such connections or equipment for other than educational purposes. While access policies are necessary they need to be audited routinely to ensure their effectiveness which is explained in the next chapter, "Auditing Policy."

QUESTIONS

1. What are some emerging problems with the way employees are using their computers at work?

2. What is meant by purpose and intent in the access policy?

3. Describe logon and password complexities.

4. Explain what is meant by rights and privileges.

VIGNETTE CHAPTER 6   Am I a Criminal?

Located in the southern mid-west part of the United States is the Sunny Dale School District which boasts high student achievement and low teacher turnover. Michael is a 10th grade Mathematics teacher at Blackwell High School. He has worked for the Sunny Dale School District for 11 years. The teachers are paid about $10,000 less than the nearest school district. Because of hard economic times, budgets are being cut and the district is chopping away at benefits.

At a family function, Michael was asked by his cousin if he wanted to make up that $10,000 in lost wages. He explained that it could be done in several seconds and he had little to no risk of getting caught. He wanted Michael to gather 100 student names, dates of birth, addresses, and social security numbers and transfer them to a jump drive, a high-speed small storage device by using three simple commands, Control + A, Control + C, and Control + V. The first command would highlight all the school records, the second command would copy them all, and the last command would paste all the records into the jump drive in seconds. He would just have to close out the screen, remove the jump drive, and leave with the data.

Michael told his cousin that he would have the data by the end of the day. On Monday during his planning period, Michael captured the data and pasted it on his jump drive. He exited the program and stored the jump drive in his case. That night Michael met with his cousin and traded the information for the money. Michael was unaware that his cousin would have fake IDs and credit cards made from the data and make over $100,000 in the next month from the stolen personal data.

Because it was easy to do the first time, Michael decided to steal the password of a fellow math teacher. Michael looked over his friend's shoulder when he signed on, and remembered the password. The next day, Michael went to the media center to avoid using his own computer, signed on as the other teacher, and took the data from the files. Michael did the same with other teachers' logons and passwords from their computers. He also used his home computer. Over the course of four months, Michael did this four more times and made a total of over $50,000. One spring day the FBI showed up at the school, took Michael into custody, and charged him with numerous counts of conspiracy to commit identity theft/credit card fraud. He was also charged under the Rico Statute for criminal enterprise.

Following the arrest, the school district requested that the government agencies share advice about protecting data and limiting the chances that the same thing could occur again. The FBI agents discussed password and logon requirements and complexities. They also explained how someone looking over your shoulder would have trouble remembering complex numbers, letters, and characters. They discussed monitoring and auditing network access logons from different and unusual locations, and they explained how this could alert the district network administrator. Another simple network setting could be used to limit logon hours and restrict access to certain locations. The most important suggestion was to assign limited rights and privileges to teachers so they would not have full access to all student information.

QUESTIONS

1. What policies should the school district revisit and change?

2. Who is at fault for this breach in security?

3. Could this happen at your school or district?

4. How often should you revisit technology policies?

5. If you were representing the school district would you call for a full audit?

6. Give examples from recent news articles where identify theft has occurred.

ACTIVITY

1. In small group discussions identify from the list of stakeholders below the individuals that are affected by the dilemma in the vignette and brainstorm ways they can affect change.

2. How do they communicate and in what forum?

3. Discuss your school or district's written plan of action for this problem, if one exists.

4. Identify any resources that could be utilized to resolve this dilemma.

5. Have one person in your group take notes and share your group's findings in front of the class after the discussion.

6. Organize the consensus.

Outside Government Agencies	Outside Technology Professionals
Parents	Crisis Team
Principals	Outside Private Agencies
Staff	School Lawyers
Students	Counselor
Superintendent	School Board
Teachers	Media (TV, Radio, Internet)
Technology Personnel	State's Attorney

Chapter 7

Auditing Policy

The auditing policy is addressed in the Risk Assessment Checklist and Profile Instrument. This chapter gives educational leaders the knowledge and ability to interpret data access.

KEY CONCEPTS
Data protection
Equipment
Data auditing
Technology plans

OBJECTIVES
1. List the reasons the auditing policy protects data.
2. Explain "non-physical threats."
3. Make a list of the data that should be audited by the IT security manager.

RELATED ELCC STANDARDS
Standard 1.0
Standard 3.0
Standard 5.0

INTRODUCTION

Every institution of learning should have acceptable use policies for both the students attending the institution and staff members. Many non-educational organizations have acceptable use policies addressing how often data can be accessed. Policies can also address how privileges are lost, and for how long. They can also be written to address the protection of data and ownership of software. Educational leaders should recognize that these policies are important for the TCO of the technology Additionally. leaders must recognize the institution's ability to continue with its daily, short-term, and long-term activities, all of which hinge on data protection.

As computers have become more accessible, the type and amount of data stored has become a concern. The loss of school district, company, or government information has become a major disaster for the United States. Robinson (2010) stated the *U.S. Information Security Law, Part 1* (Computer Fraud and Abuse Act (CFAA)) protects all local educational agencies (LEAs) from any non-physical threat to the organization's integrity and the availability of the data systems. The Digital Millennium Copyright Act (DMCA) contains provisions for protecting copyright of an owner of technology. The law also requires each state to develop and enforce laws legislation that fills the gaps between CFAA and DMCA. Cyclical audits of organizational technology require auditing all members, regardless of their position.

Many transactions that occur—especially for commerce—are completed via computer. Contracts, solicitation of contract bids, as well as banking activities take place using the computer through access to the World Wide Web. Conrad (2010) from Demand Media argued it is critical for educational leaders to understand the importance of securing not just student data, but all data within the jurisdiction of the school district or college. Security policies are as necessary for state and local organizations as they are for large organizations and government agencies (Conrad, 2010).

DATA PROTECTION

Local educational agencies must comply with various regulatory compliance and security requirements that safeguard unauthorized access to sensitive data from outsiders as well as staff members of the organization who do not have a "need to know." The network administrator is responsible for controlling access to the network. Whether the data is confidential or sensitive, stored on site, off site, or in a central location, data protection is necessary. There are many software companies and standalone information technicians offering data security or willing to develop data security tailored to the school or district's needs.

The SANS Institute (2006) determined that individual schools should arrange for a meeting with the technology manager to prepare for an information security audit before the allocation of funds or any payment is paid to a data security auditor. The meeting objective is to provide the educational leader with an update of the condition of the district's technology security. The IT manager and the network administrator provide a document identifying organizational data, storage location, and any additional information, which may include:

1. Status of current concerns.
2. New concerns.

3. Original copies of documents ensuring compliance and/or certifications required by all regulatory agencies.
4. Current user security features, login and password protection for each level of protection.
5. Login audits.
6. Breaches of security.
7. Review of the LEA's audit vulnerability policy.

At the minimum, the audit vulnerability policy should begin with a statement of the purpose of the policy, which may or may not contain an agreement between an internal and/or external auditing company and the school district. The objectives of the audit should reflect and/or support the goals of the organization to protect the students and all employees from access to stated information. The audit vulnerability policy addresses all concerns including, but not limited to, updates to federal, state, and/or local regulations, security software, and current or new computer technology equipment. If a breach in information security is found, the policy should have an inclusion statement of what the auditors can and cannot do, such as denying service to any member.

The audit policy for vulnerability establishes boundaries for the auditors. If an interruption of service occurs, the policy should clearly identify the responsibilities of the organization and auditor. The names and contact information for the managers and the auditor should be documented in this policy.

EQUIPMENT

Auditing and understanding vulnerability remains a challenge to all K-12 organizations at the district and building levels. In fact, many states require a technology audit of any state-funded equipment. Many districts and schools have limited audits related to software, and current or new computer technology equipment. Auditing policy can address the accountability of physical equipment through inventories as well. This is discussed further in Chapter 8.

DATA AUDITING

Data auditing is somewhat complex but understanding best practices and utilizing a "data auditing framework" allows educational leaders, according to Jones and Ball (2008), "a mechanism for collecting such information through its audit methodology." There are benefits to this methodology such as data risk management, data asset identification, and planning. Since this is a policy unique to the organizational culture, "the Data Audit Framework is a first step in this process, assisting organizations to collect such information so they can develop policies and processes appropriate to their needs" (p. 113). This framework has four stages:

1. Planning the audit
2. Identifying and classifying assets
3. Assessing management of data assets.
4. Reporting and recommending.

> In the planning stage the purpose and scope of the audit are defined. Preliminary research is conducted and meetings scheduled so time spent with the organization's staff can be optimized. The purpose of the second stage is to establish what data assets exist and to classify them according to their value to the organization. The classification step determines the scope of further audit activities, as only the vital or most significant assets are assessed in greater detail in the following stage. The information collected in Stage 3 helps to identify weaknesses in data policy and current data creation procedures. This provides a basis of recommendations in the final stage of the audit. The knowledge gained from the audit will enable the organization to improve its data management policies and processes. (p. 114)

We recommend that K-12 organizational leaders protect their data and equipment assets with data management systems software which include a physical inventory system. These systems are software programs that are easy to manage and interrupt and may be somewhat overpriced but in the long run will protect and manage your most valuable assets. The function of data and equipment management/auditing can also be outsourced and considered as part of the TCO for technology.

TECHNOLOGY PLANS

Technology planning is highly recommended in both the short and the long term. Short-term planning should include the TCO concepts while long-term planning should be more comprehensive in nature. Comprehensive technology plans include many aspects of technology. They should (but many do not) include inventory and auditing policies. These comprehensive plans are mentioned in the U.S. Department of Education Office of Planning, Evaluation and Policy Development, publication *State Strategies and Practices for Educational Technology: Volume I—Examining the Enhancing Education through Technology Program*.

> This report is part of the U.S. Department of Education's National Educational Technology Trends Study (NETTS). It describes state strategies and practices with regard to educational technology, focusing specifically on the role of the EETT program and discusses the relationships of state and local technology program. (p. 22)

Early technologists believe:

> Schools that effectively use technology have a carefully designed technology plan that is a part of the overall school-improvement plan. A technology plan that is not integral to the overall improvement plan is likely to be short-lived (Cradler, 1996). As part of the school-improvement plan, technology should support the curricular goals of the school. "Technology is neither an end in itself nor an add-on," notes the Office of Educational Technology (1994c). "It is a tool for improving— and ultimately, transforming—teaching and learning. To accomplish that job, technology must be an integral part of [the] school or community's overall plan to move all children toward high academic standards.

Modern technologists like those that developed the Missouri Department of Education's (2011) plans from best practices believe in forming a technology planning committee with members reflecting all the stakeholders. These modern designers plan in steps:

1. Select a well-rounded technology committee.
2. Develop a technology mission statement.
3. Collect and evaluate technology raw data.
4. Develop technology goals and objectives.
5. Develop and implement an action plan and timelines.
6. Disseminate, monitor, and evaluate the technology plan.

Furthermore, the technology mission statement, vision, goals, and objectives should be aligned with your state technology mission statement, vision, goals, and objectives. Chapter 2 outlined equipment costs, operation and maintenance costs, disposition costs, and non-operational costs associated with comprehensive technology planning. The Risk Assessment Checklist and Profile Instrument in Chapter 11 will give educational leaders a tool to measure the levels of cyber threat through policies governing their organization.

CONCLUSION

Every school, and perhaps every building, within the jurisdiction of the local educational agencies should have an auditing policy for securing the technology purchased and/or used to accomplish the daily, short-term, and long-term goals of the organization. Safeguarding the technology developed or purchased by the organization should be included in the district's auditing policy and procedure. Several software companies can help provide various levels of data protection;

however, internal data protection audits can greatly reduce the chances of loss or stolen data.

So far in this book we have examined intangibles. In the next chapter, we will take a look into the physical policy of tangible equipment containing valuable data.

QUESTIONS

1. What is an audit?

2. Who conducts the audit?

3. Make a list of the areas that should be audited.

VIGNETTE CHAPTER 7 Impending Doom

Mr. Franks was just hired by the Washington School District as a network security administrator. He has 20 years experience in network security from the private sector. Mr. Franks has stayed up to date with all the federal and state laws and regulations. He is considered an expert in his field.

Dr. Peterson has been the superintendent of Washington School District for the past 18 years. He is well liked and respected by his peers. He is a status quo leader and follows suit with his many friends on the Board of Education.

Mr. Franks' first order of business was to familiarize himself with the existing technology policies of the school district. He spent most of the first week reading the district's policies and visiting the schools. Mr. Franks discovered that most of the policies were outdated and in need of revision. He also discovered that there was no audit vulnerability policy which addresses all concerns including, but not limited to, updates to federal, state, and/or local regulations, security software, and current or new computer technology, and the security of data and equipment in regards to physical and non-physical threats. He met with all school principals at their schools.

Every school in the district had poor and incomplete equipment inventory lists. Equipment lacked district labels and ID numbers. There was no standardized inventory list, and all that had been done was in hard copy. Over the years each school had obtained a variety of software that came from different grants, and no one could account for all of it. The principals could not answer questions about software site licenses. Newer computers had locks on the backs of them, and older computers were not secured. Each school stored and reported data differently. They even had different forms of backing up data, but did not keep a log of when and who did the backups. Mr. Franks found a culture of technology confusion with lack of accountability.

After becoming familiar with the district's problems Mr. Franks met with the superintendent of schools, Dr. Peterson and shared these words:

> As the network administrator, I am responsible for controlling access to the network. Whether the data is confidential or sensitive, stored on site, off site, or in a central location, data protection is necessary. If we outsource, there are many software companies offering data security and some willing to develop data security tailored to the district's specific needs. It comes with a yearly price, but it is cheaper to outsource than hire several specialists to maintain such databases.

Dr. Peterson advised Mr. Franks that he would have to take this matter up with the members of the Board of Education at the next executive board meeting in a month's time. Dr. Peterson said he would get back to him and added that the district was strapped for spending. He added that due to hard economic times, the district was already cutting budgets and streamlining departments. Mr. Franks left the superintendent with these words, "It's not for me to say when a disaster is coming, but to prepare for the recovery because one always comes when you least expect it."

One month later, the superintendent called Mr. Franks in for a meeting. Dr. Peterson shared that the members of the Board of Education had rejected his idea to outsource such a project. They felt that the present system in place had worked for the last

20 years, and there was no need to fix anything if it wasn't broken. They also added that they did not see any impending doom lurking on the horizon.

QUESTIONS

How would you describe the culture of the school district?

1. Do you believe there is a shared vision?

2. What could Mr. Franks do as a change agent for technology?

3. Did the superintendent give Mr. Franks any support?

4. What is the relationship between the superintendent and the Board of Education members?

5. Describe the leadership style of the superintendent.

6. Discuss how you would come up with a shared vision for this school system.

ACTIVITY

1. In small group discussions identify from the list of stakeholders below the individuals that are affected by the dilemma in the vignette and brainstorm ways they can affect change.

2. How do they communicate and in what forum?

3. Discuss your school or district's written plan of action for this problem, if one exists.

4. Identify any resources that could be utilized to resolve this dilemma.

5. Have one person in your group take notes and share your group's findings in front of the class after the discussion.

6. Organize the consensus.

Outside Government Agencies	Outside Technology Professionals
Parents	Crisis Team
Principals	Outside Private Agencies
Staff	School Lawyers
Students	Counselor
Superintendent	School Board
Teachers	Media (TV, Radio, Internet)
Technology Personnel	State's Attorney

Chapter 8

Physical Policy

The physical policy is addressed in the Risk Assessment Checklist and Profile Instrument. This chapter gives educational leaders an awareness of equipment and data security.

KEY CONCEPTS
Secure physical access to network equipment
Random audits
Inventory worksheet

OBJECTIVES
1. Describe secure physical network and equipment
2. Describe secure data and explain how secure data relates to the physical policy.
3. List all types of storage devices including handheld drives and their threats to an organization's data.

RELATED ELCC STANDARDS
Standard 3.0
Standard 5.0

INTRODUCTION

In addition to completing an audit of the organizational information and data protection systems, schools and districts must complete physical audits of software, networks, and hardware. One of the most important information security concerns facing educational leaders is the organization's network. The network and its access should be continually audited. Part of that auditing system is the monitoring of the use of personal user identifications, passwords, and other authentication systems. For example, the U.S. Department of Education and the U.S. Department of Agriculture have a very comprehensive physical security standard for IT. The policy addresses the use of various types of computer equipment, software, and access to the software as well as accessing areas that house networks and work areas. The policy also addresses having an 'Emergency Plan' (U.S. Department of Agriculture, 2011). The general IT restrictions section should provide guidance concerning maintenance and audit. Since the invention of the microchip, organizations have invested in different advance technology equipment such as smartphones, laptops, notebooks, and cell phones.

SECURE PHYSICAL ACCESS TO NETWORK EQUIPMENT

All of this equipment costs money. Depending on the physical size of an organization, it may be a wise investment to hire a technician whose job it is to monitor IT equipment. All of the technology equipment a school district purchases should be labeled with some sort of physical identification and recorded by the IT department. A spreadsheet or other document should be used to identify each employee, their work location, and what routers and/or servers exist at that workstation to provide technology. Any and all technology equipment in the employee's office and/or assigned to them to work outside the work environment should also be recorded.

RANDOM AUDITS

Each district should ensure that the IT department conducts random audits of the equipment and its location. This is done by identifying tagged equipment and matching the identification number first assigned to the equipment with a printed hardcopy. Many states require a yearly inventory of a school district's technology because of federal and state funding for accountability. The audit also allows the IT manager to become aware of equipment that may not be in operating condition or that has been lost. The organization's administrator must ensure that the building itself is secure, and each office and/or room is secure. These audits should identify whether wiring closets and central processing units (CPUs) are secured and locked. The audits should also obtain the list of employees authorized to remove equipment from the property. Any and all computer equipment removed from the property with authorization should not contain any organizational information. With the invention of high-speed data transfer devices such as thumb or jump drives, organizations and school districts should strongly consider if it is necessary to control all information from a central server and/or to disable the universal bus (USB) ports on the CPUs.

As a district or building administrator, it's important to be able to answer the following general questions:

1. Do all your computers have locks?
2. Is your wiring closet secure and temperature controlled?
3. Is there a water-generated fire sprinkler system in your computer labs?
4. Is your wiring closet, in your server closet? Why water?
5. Is there a sign out list for equipment?
6. Is your technology inventory up to date?
7. Can your teachers, administrators, or staff access school data via smartphone?
8. Is there a maintenance audit?
9. Do you have a short-term and long-term technology plan that reflects the TCO?

We recommend a technology inventory database system with hardcopy worksheets to control for damage, theft, and faulty equipment and programs. One source we recommend offers a free download, "Technology Inventory Worksheet," in pdf or Word and it is very extensive. The source is called *techsoup*, the technology place for nonprofits. They can be found at http://www.techsoup. org/learningcenter/techplan/archives/page9808.cfm. They have one of the most comprehensive technology worksheets on the Web to record and monitor a school and district's technology inventory. However, we recommend a simple technology asset inventory worksheet. The hard copy will allow a simple guide for a database creation. The items included are the most basic but the most important for inventory control.

INVENTORY WORKSHEET

TABLE 8.1 Technology Asset Inventory Worksheet

Equipment	Condition	Comments/Recommendations
Make		
Model		
Equipment Serial Number		
District Identification Number		
Assignment/Location/School		
Funds Used to Purchase		

Software Installed

1.

2.

3.

4.

5.

6.

7.

8.

9.

10.

Replacement Scheduled

Person Conducting Inventory

Date of this Inventory

Ultimately, it is the building administrator's responsibility to schedule, monitor, and report the findings of school technology audits. This includes missing and damaged hardware. In many cases there is no audit of software. Knowing what software there is outside the normal allowed computer software is highly important for the building administrator. In Chapter 14 we address fair use and copyright laws. In many cases schools have obtained grants which include specialty software which is installed on computers for student use. Understanding site licensing and maintaining an inventory of software is priority. However, in many schools and districts this has become a sleeping tiger. Lawsuits and the loss of funding are a result of lack of accountability of software.

CONCLUSION

The physical environment includes the secure physical network and equipment, the securing of data, and how secure data relates to the physical policy. Understanding tangibles as hardware and intangibles as software is important for educational leaders in this age of accountability and valuable in planning the future of the organization's technology expenditures. It also protects against all types of storage devices including handheld drives and their threats to an organization's data. The next chapter relates to internal audits and analysis.

QUESTIONS

1. What is a physical policy?

2. List tangible and intangible technologies physical policy should consider.

3. How do high-speed data transfer devices relate to physical policies?

VIGNETTE CHAPTER 8   Information for the Taking

Billings High School is located in a prosperous school district outside of Washington, DC. The school is profoundly funded and lacks for nothing. They have maintained high assessment scores consistently for 5 years. The number of students entering college upon graduation is 92 percent. Dr. Long has been the principal at the high school for the past ten years.

Assistant Superintendent Ms. Chung has 3 years experience in her position. Her peers describe her as a strong participative leader who closely follows policies.

One evening Ms. Chung received a disturbing call from Dr. Long. While at dinner with his family, his school laptop was stolen from his car. Ms. Chung asked if there was any school sensitive information on the laptop that could expose any employee, staff, or student personal identifiers. Dr. Long explained that he had been working on staff files which contained names, addresses, contact numbers, dates of birth, and social security numbers. There were also some old files containing letters to parents about student behavior and other letters to businesses regarding fundraising.

Dr. Long filed a police report about the incident. He told the police that the information on the computer could not be accessed because the laptop was password protected. The officer explained that for only $49 you can purchase password removal downloadable software from the Internet for any Windows product.

The next day Dr. Long met with Ms. Chung at the central office. At the meeting, Ms. Chung provided him with a copy of the Employee Acceptable Use Policy, signed by him just the previous year. There was a sub-section that forbids any sensitive data to leave the premises of any properties owned by the school district. Additionally, the sub-section defined and outlined what data is considered sensitive, which included any and all personal identifiers. Ms. Chung explained that the district takes the violation of these policies very seriously and regards the protection of data as a high priority.

Ms. Chung asked Dr. Long to explain why he did not follow this policy. Dr. Long boldly stated, "My vehicle is alarmed, the laptop was secured and password protected." He continued to add that every principal he knows of takes their school-issued laptop home to do school related work in the evenings and on weekends. He even told her his insurance would cover the expense of the loss. Ms. Chung explained that all school business off property should be conducted online using the district's secure portal, which requires a logon, password, and site keys identification. Ms. Chung thanked Dr. Long for coming and ended the meeting.

The next day Ms. Chung and the school district's resource security supervisor entered Billings High School and confronted Dr. Long in his office. Ms. Chung handed him a dismissal letter and instructed Dr. Long to gather his personal belongings and surrender his keys. He was escorted from the property. The assistant principal was directed to assume the temporary duties of the principal until further notice.

QUESTIONS

1. Describe what is meant by secure physical network and equipment.

2. Describe secure data and explain how secure data relates to the physical policy.

3. List all types of storage devices including handheld drives and determine their threats to an organization's data.

4. Write a policy regarding the use of equipment leaving school property.

ACTIVITY

1. In small group discussions identify from the list of stakeholders below the individuals that are affected by the dilemma in the vignette and brainstorm ways they can affect change.

2. How do they communicate and in what forum?

3. Discuss your school or district's written plan of action for this problem, if one exists.

4. Identify any resources that could be utilized to resolve this dilemma.

5. Have one person in your group take notes and share your group's findings in front of the class after the discussion.

6. Organize the consensus.

Outside Government Agencies	Outside Technology Professionals
Parents	Crisis Team
Principals	Outside Private Agencies
Staff	School Lawyers
Students	Counselor
Superintendent	School Board
Teachers	Media (TV, Radio, Internet)
Technology Personnel	State's Attorney

Chapter 9

Analysis Policy

The analysis policy is addressed in the Risk Assessment Checklist and Profile Instrument. This chapter provides educational leaders with an understanding of internal and external cyber security.

KEY CONCEPTS
Open network ports
TCP packet analysis
OS Hardening
Router security
Firewall systems (access control list)
Encryption (IP security) (Point-to-Point Tunneling Protocol)
Network address translation
Intrusion detection/prevention system, virus, Malware,
   Worm, Spyware, Backdoor, spam, pop-up protection
Disaster recovery plan on or off site

OBJECTIVES
1. List and explain the many functions of the analysis policy.
2. Determine and discuss the importance of maintaining the security of a system's infrastructure from outside threats.
3. Compare operation system hardening and router security and the importance of both.
4. List and describe the best practices of firewalls.

RELATED ELCC STANDARDS
Standard 3.0
Standard 5.0

INTRODUCTION

When considering external access to school district technology infrastructure, the dangers of the Internet are always present. This is an ever-changing environment that school leaders cannot ignore. For example, compared to a decade ago, according to Web security firm Breach Security, the number of systems that are being accessed improperly is rising rapidly. In the first two business quarters of 2009, the number of security incidents related to Web applications rose 30 percent over the same time in 2008. Attacks against government and education systems account for 17 percent of all reported hacking incidents.

In the last 20 years, school districts have invested over $40 billion in technology infrastructure, professional development, and technical support. Keeping that investment and the private information safe is the responsibility of each individual system operator. The need to develop, implement, and follow policies for computer system safety in educational systems is well documented. Policies dictating acceptable use, access, authentication, downloads, and auditing and physical usage have become part of standard operating procedures. One policy that continues to grow and change as technology grows is analysis policy. Analysis policy consists of the following predetermined technology standards to maintain the security of a system's infrastructure from outside threats. The standards that need to be maintained include:

- Open network port maintenance.
- Transmission Control Protocol packet analysis.
- Operating System Hardening.
- Router security.
- Firewall system maintenance.
- Encryption development.
- Network address translation.
- Intrusion detection/prevention systems.
- Virus/Malware protection.

When maintained properly, each standard can contribute to a wall of impenetrability around an educational system's technology infrastructure. These best practices will be exampled in each key concept.

OPEN NETWORK PORTS

Ports are the "openings" or doorways through which applications on a system's computer can reach the software on a system server. Web pages and data transfer software require their respective ports to be "open" on the system's Internet server to be publicly accessible. The standard port for http or Internet Web page access is port 80. The standard port for email access is port 25. There are hundreds of ports that make up a system's Internet access and can be opened and closed by a system administrator when needed. Monitoring and maintaining the number of open ports and preventing non-authorized access to a system through an unintentional open port is the essence of this component of the overall analysis policy.

Protecting open posts is also a network security priority for the IT manager. Cisco Systems warns that an attacker can mount a DoS (Denial of Service) attack on a functional or operating port. An attacker (or attackers) will flood a port with more requests than the system can handle, forcing it to shut down and deny all requests for service. Cisco Systems' best practices recommend applying internal port security, which allows the system to build a list of acceptable addresses that are allowed to access the port. For best practices, this prevents an attacker from flooding a port with requests in an attempt to maliciously shut down the port.

TCP PACKET ANALYSIS

TCP stands for Transmission Control Protocol and is the component of a system infrastructure that accepts data from a data stream and breaks it into chunks called "packets," which move in and out of a system's network. A packet consists of all the information being transferred including a header, the part that identifies the sender. Being able to analyze the information in the packets reveals where the data is coming from and can assist in preventing harmful data from entering the network. Best practices includes using a "sniffer" program like Wireshark that allows a system administrator to capture TCP packets coming into a network so he/she can identify the author of a packet, thereby being able to identify malicious data, .exes, or programs. Techtarget.com's best practices suggest using Wireshark to: (1) monitor the current status of the network and get a handle on system performance, (2) peer into the communications to pinpoint the cause of problems quickly and accurately, and (3) identify problems at the packet level before the problem turns system wide.

OS HARDENING

OS-Hardening stands for operating system hardening and dictates that protecting the operating system requires system administrators to install and maintain updates and service patches. Forrester Research, Incorporated suggests best practices for OS Hardening goes further and recommends that administrators:

- Install operating systems and system components from approved authoring sources.

- Remove or disable unnecessary or outdated system components.
- Uninstall any unnecessary or outdated software.
- Set security parameters, file protections, and enable audit logging.
- Disable or change the passwords of default accounts.
- Install approved anti-virus software.

Best practices dictate that all upgrades be applied and tested on a ghost operating system first prior to updating the operational operating system.

ROUTER SECURITY

A router can be likened to an Internet post office. Thousands of bits of information come into a system and the router reads the address information, and then decides the destination. Routers also help system members navigate their pathways within the network. Considering the amount of information that comes into a router, it is greatly prone to attack or to be a gateway for harmful or malicious attacks. Cisco Systems recommends best practices for routers include:

- Securing the system router to prevent someone from walking up and performing a password reset.
- Locking down the router with administrative passwords.
- Backing up the router configurations in a decentralized source in case reconfiguration of the router is needed.
- Locking down all switches and wireless access with passwords.

Additional best practices for router security include: (a) creating a diagram of the network so a map exists to assist in visualizing the entire system, (b) protecting the router with a firewall and access control lists (ACLs), (c) creating an automated system that changes passwords on a periodic basis, (d) making passwords complex by utilizing numbers, letters, and symbols, and (e) encrypting sensitive network traffic by using Secure Shell (SSH) or Secure Network Management Protocol (SNMP) encryption.

FIREWALL SYSTEMS

A firewall is designed to grant or deny access to network transmissions based on rules put in place by a system administrator. There are three main types of firewalls: network layer, application layer, and proxies. All three essentially operate in the same fashion; they monitor TCP/IP traffic and only let through data that has been defined by a system administration set of rules. Linda Musthaler of Networkworld recommends that best practices for safe firewall operation include:

- Documenting all firewall rule changes so system administrators can have a record of momentary changes and mandated changes.
- Installing all access rules with minimal access rights.
- Verifying that every firewall access rule change meets the needs of the entire security policy as compared to a single need.
- Removing unused or outdated firewall rules.
- Performing an annual firewall review to delete redundant, outdated, and temporary access rules.

ENCRYPTION

Encryption is the process of converting information to make it unreadable to anyone except those that have a key or decoder. For system administrators, encrypting and decrypting system traffic is an essential component for preventing hackers from obtaining information to fuel attacks. While there are a multitude of encryption standards available, the key to encryption is determining what information on a system needs to be encrypted. While some systems choose to encrypt only information deemed sensitive or email communication, Sophos Systems best practices suggest that all system information be encrypted to heighten the safety factor (Sophos Security Topics, 2011). Encrypting all information data, when it enters the system as a document or other file, protects all information in the case of theft. The two main encrypting processes include Ipsec, which encrypts data at the packet level, and Point-to-Point Tunneling Protocol, which encrypts information over Virtual Private Networks or intranets.

NETWORK ADDRESS TRANSLATION

Network address translation (NAT) modifies the network IP address information while it is in transit through the system routers. NAT translates personal system address information to a public address that represents the company-wide address and hides all internal IP address information.

INTRUSION DETECTION/PREVENTION SYSTEM

Intrusion detection/prevention system (IDPS) monitors all the events happening in a computer system or network and analyzes them for possible violations of or threats to security policies, acceptable use policies, or standard security practices. IDPS is intended to identify, log, and prevent system incidents while reporting the incidents to system administrators. IDPS has become the popular way to protect system-wide architecture for large infrastructures. There are four types of IDPS: (1) network-based which monitors network segments or devices, (2) wireless which monitors wireless systems for suspicious traffic, (3) network behavior analysis (NBA) which monitors network traffic for unusual traffic flow, and (4) host-based which monitors a single host for suspicious activity. Symantec Technologies Incorporated's best practices for IDPS include: (1) the use of multiple types or all four kinds of IDPS technologies to create a comprehensive protection base, (2) working with IDPS technologies that are capable of integrating with the other programs aforementioned, and (3) defining the system IDPS needs before purchasing the technology.

DISASTER RECOVERY PLAN

All system administrators need to develop a disaster recovery program in the event of a natural or human-induced disaster. The key to disaster recovery is backing up the data in multiple ways to cover multiple disaster possibilities or needs. Perhaps the best and most widely adopted disaster recovery strategy is known as GFS (Grandfather, Father, Son) where system data is backed up in three ways. "Grandfather" consists of a monthly, off-site backup of system data and applications. "Father" consists of a weekly backup of system data and applications and can be done on site or off site. "Son" consists of a daily on-site backup of system data and applications. Daily backups can be either differential (a backup of all changes made since the last full backup) or incremental (a backup of only the additions to data since the last backup).

CONCLUSION

The sources cited in this chapter are well-known established industry leaders in best practices for technologies. Overall, an effective system analysis policy requires system administrators who know the smallest details of the network and the technology. The system administrator needs to be attentive to both internal and external threats to keep the data protected and flowing. They should meet with and report results to district and building administrators to keep them informed. The next chapter examines the protection of privacy while using electronic equipment. In later chapters we will also examine copyright and fair use.

QUESTIONS

1. What is an analysis policy?

2. List tangible and intangible technologies that should be considered in an analysis policy.

3. How do backups relate to analysis policies?

VIGNETTE CHAPTER 9 Freebies

Brandy Heights School District is located in an urban community just outside of a major city in the Southwest. On Monday morning, schools across the district experienced a series of network disruptions. These disruptions had an effect on the software responsible for grading, attendance, scheduling, tracking, and guidance. Computer workstations locked up and froze while teachers were grading or posting attendance. Scheduling and tracking programs were not accessible, and the guidance department computers showed a screen that forced you to purchase Spyware to remove the detected Spyware. Clearly, something destructive had infiltrated and contaminated the network.

Mr. Willis, the network administrator, initiated a full investigation into the occurrence, which included packet analysis. The analysis revealed that a bundle or blended threat had entered the network through a software program. The intrusion had been reported at several schools in the district during the prior week.

All principals and assistant principals attended an emergency meeting at the district office. Mr. Willis explained:

> Worms replicate within your network and can interrupt transmissions by using bandwidth. They can travel across networks to intranets and extranets. On the other hand, Trojan Horse first appears to be a useful and necessary program, but once downloaded causes damage. Trojans are capable of deleting files, hindering and damaging programs, and creating a backdoor or rear entrance into your school's network for intruders. Blended threats are a combination of malicious coding using Worms and Trojans together. That's what we are dealing with here.

Through interviews with teachers and administrators, Mr. Willis uncovered the reason for the breach. A group of teachers from the Brandy Heights School District had attended a graduate class at a local university. A week ago, the class had a guest speaker who talked about the integration of technology in the classroom. The speaker was an instructional technology specialist who discussed enhancements to support curriculum and capture the interest of students. The speaker demonstrated the use of portable applications for the teachers. With the use of the portable applications, teachers could create instructional WebQuests and PowerPoints with both video and audio clips. The instructional specialist demonstrated how to download freebies from the Internet and how to use portable applications in classrooms during instruction. That evening several of the teachers used jump drives to download the free applications. The next day they used the applications to enhance instruction and began sharing jump drives with other teachers. At one school's faculty meeting, teachers from the graduate class shared the new use of technology with all of the teachers in the building. Soon, portable applications were being used in every school in the district.

These facts were shared at the emergency meeting of school district administrators, and Mr. Willis explained:

> Intrusion Detection Prevention Systems for virus, Malware, Worm, Spyware, Backdoor, spam, and pop-up protection were in place in our district. However secure, it was not set up to scan flash drives and any and all programs contained within them. The new threats to systems today are portable apps, programs such

as Freeware, which run off of flash drives. These programs run as full programs allowing access to the Internet through border managers and firewalls. Most of these Freeware and portable apps programs are legitimate software, but in some cases they are malicious programs which bundle Worms and Trojans.

QUESTIONS

1. Discuss in class your understanding of IDPS.

2. Make a list of IDPS threads.

3. Describe how portable application programs work.

ACTIVITY

1. In small group discussions identify from the list of stakeholders below the individuals that are affected by the dilemma in the vignette and brainstorm ways they can affect change.

2. How do they communicate and in what forum?

3. Discuss your school or district's written plan of action for this problem, if one exists.

4. Identify any resources that could be utilized to resolve this dilemma.

5. Have one person in your group take notes and share your group's findings in front of the class after the discussion.

6. Organize the consensus.

Outside Government Agencies	Outside Technology Professionals
Parents	Crisis Team
Principals	Outside Private Agencies
Staff	School Lawyers
Students	Counselor
Superintendent	School Board
Teachers	Media (TV, Radio, Internet)
Technology Personnel	State's Attorney

Chapter 10

Privacy Policy

The privacy policy is addressed in the Risk Assessment Checklist and Profile Instrument. This chapter explains to educational leaders the legal aspects of access.

KEY CONCEPTS
U.S. Patriot Act
Privacy statement
Procedural and substantive rights

OBJECTIVES
1. Relate how today's privacy policy is derived from the Privacy Act of 1974.
2. Develop and list the reasons the Privacy Act requires any agency or organization that is maintaining a system of records to give an individual access to any records they might have about an individual.
3. Describe how a privacy policy relates to the Patriot Act.

RELATED ELCC STANDARDS
Standard 3.0
Standard 5.0

INTRODUCTION

The Privacy Act of 1974 was created in response to concerns about how the formation and use of computerized databases might impact individuals' privacy rights. The privacy policy is a legal document that discloses and manages a customer's or employee's data, personal information, or professional identification. All privacy policies are different, depending upon the organization.

The privacy policy intends to protect all important and personal information related to an employee or student. Even though a privacy policy is used often in schools, businesses, or other professional organizations, there is no universal method in creating a privacy policy document. For the educational leader a privacy policy should be established in the interest of safeguarding the collection, access, use, dissemination, and storage of personal identifiable information.

The courts have stated that privacy rights in conjunction with communications do not extend to employees using company-owned computer systems, even in situations where employees have password-protected accounts. Legal incidents where employers have monitored their employees' electronic transmissions involving email, Internet, and computer-file usage on company-owned equipment have not been ruled as invasion of privacy. Such actions as "invasion of privacy" do not provide employees with additional protection.

The Privacy Act of 1974 only covers U.S. citizens and permanent residents, meaning only a citizen or permanent resident can sue under the Privacy Act. The Privacy Act protects records that can be retrieved by other parties without permission such as a name, social security number, birth date, address, or other identifiable information. The Act only protects and covers records in the possession and control of federal agencies. An individual is allowed access to his/her records and has permission to request the records if applicable (Services, 2011). It prohibits disclosure of these records without the written consent of the individual to whom the records pertain unless otherwise stated in the Act. All records are held within the Privacy Act systems and under security, which is published in the Federal Register. The Federal Register can publish a notice to identify the legal authority for collecting and storing of all records.

U.S. PATRIOT ACT

The U.S. Patriot Act expanded the federal government's authority to monitor the communications and Internet activities of individuals, including emails and pictures. The U.S. Patriot Act was signed into law by President George W. Bush on October 26, 2001 just after 9/11. The federal government consistently maintains a large amount of databases on individual people. As society became more technology efficient, it became easier for agencies to cross-reference personal data of individual people (Center, 2010). Citizens and legislators became more aware that if the information were to be compiled, it could be abused. In a technological era computers are able to search files quickly and easily (Center, 2010). Since, a person's life could be compiled into a single database in a matter of minutes, it was vital to embark a privacy act policy.

The Privacy Act of 1974 not only secures the personal information and identification of employees and customers, it manages the roles and responsibilities under certain statutes and programs (Agency, 2010). The United States does not have specific federal regulation for establishing a universal implementation of privacy policies. It is totally up to organizations to establish a privacy policy for their employees and customers. Congress has considered creating laws for regulating the collection of personal information and identification, but none of the laws has been enacted. In some cases, organizations have pledged to provide a privacy policy for their employees and customers, but have not done so. Privacy policies prohibit unfair and deceptive marketing practices.

PRIVACY STATEMENT

The Privacy Policy applies to all employees, managers, and grantees working on behalf of the organization by handling and controlling access to documents, records, or systems that contain personal identifiable information (Agency, 2010). Some websites define their privacy policies by allowing browsers to automatically assess the level of privacy offered on that particular site (Privacy Policy, 2011). However, these technical solutions do not guarantee websites that adhere to the privacy policies that are dispensed on the website. Congress understood that certain governmental activities were not willing to follow the individual rights provided in the Privacy Act, such as criminal investigation documents. Some government agencies can exempt themselves from participating in certain types of record systems required by the Privacy Act. Government agencies that are engaged in law enforcement can excuse themselves from the Act's rules, but all agencies are required to publish a System of Records Notice in the Federal Register. Executive departments, military departments, independent regulatory agencies, and government-controlled corporations are all covered by the Act. This means that government-controlled companies like the U.S. Postal Service should be covered as well as the military and executive agencies like the Department of Education, the FDA, and FBI.

The Privacy Act of 1974 requires that all organizations create and maintain a System of Records Notices. A system of records consists of any item, collection, or grouping of information about an individual (Services, 2011). The System of Records Notices must be completed upon the establishment of an organization. A system of records is defined as any group of records where information is retrieved by the name of the individual or by an individual identifier (Center, 2010). In order to prevent the existence of secret databases, agencies must publish the details of all their systems of records in the Federal Register. The publication must cover intended uses of the system, and allow for interested persons to submit written data, views, or arguments to the agency. Any time that an agency wishes to establish or significantly change a system of records, it must also notify in advance the Committee on Government Operations of the House of Representatives, the Committee on Governmental Affairs of the

Senate, and the Office of Management and Budget (Center, 2010). Databases and collections of records that do not allow retrieval of information on particular individuals are not included.

PROCEDURAL AND SUBSTANTIVE RIGHTS

The Privacy Act requires the maintenance of privacy through creating four procedural and substantive rights in personal information: (1) it requires government agencies to show an individual any records kept on him/her, (2) it requires agencies to follow certain principles, called "fair information practices," when gathering and handling personal data, (3) it places restrictions on how agencies can share an individual's data with other people and agencies, and 4) individuals can sue the government for violating its provisions (Center, 2010).

The Privacy Act requires any agency or organization that is maintaining a system of records to give an individual access to any records it might have about him/her (Center, 2010). Every individual has an opportunity to review, analyze, and make copies of their record. If the individual insists that their record has an error and needs to be corrected the agency must respond to their request within ten business days, either by making the requested changes or by telling the person why they have refused to alter his record (Center, 2010). Any agency that has records on an individual must keep accurate accounts of when and to whom personal records were disclosed (Center, 2010). Personal records include: a social security number, full name, address, and birth date. These accounts should be kept for 5 years, or the lifetime of the record, whichever is longer (Center, 2010).

CONCLUSION

One of the most important aspects of the Privacy Act is that it restricts the sharing of information between government agencies (Center, 2010). Privacy protection in electronic communications has several exemptions that limit the ability to provide protection in the workplace. Privacy protection limits "matching programs," which it defines as the computerized comparison of databases in order to determine the status, rights, or benefits of the individuals within the systems of records (Center, 2010). If an agency sharing information believes that the recipient agency is not abiding by all of the necessary regulations, it cannot disclose any records to the recipient agency (Center, 2010). The matching agreement cannot be renewed unless the recipient agency certifies that it has complied with all of the provisions of the matching agreement, and the source agency has no reason to believe that this certification is inaccurate (Center, 2010). The next chapter contains the instrument and a field experience that scores your district or building knowledge of existing policies.

QUESTIONS

1. What is the intent of the privacy policy?

2. Who uses privacy policies?

3. How does the privacy policy relate to the Privacy Act of 1974?

4. How does the privacy policy relate to the Patriot Act?

VIGNETTE CHAPTER 10 Invasion of Privacy?

Cherry Hill Elementary School is a well-run school in the suburbs of a small city. Mike Parker is a veteran principal at Cherry Hill Elementary School. He has been principal for 11 years. Brian Weller has been a 5th grade teacher at the school for the past 8 years.

Brian Weller had been going through a very nasty divorce and custody battle with his separated wife. For the past six months Weller had been late for work numerous times and had to leave early and take off frequently to be at court and meet with his lawyers. Weller had been seen out on the weekends with a young female teacher, and it was reported that he was drinking heavily.

Mr. Parker conducted an investigation on behalf of the school based on recent observations and information he had received about Weller. Mr. Parker asked the technology manager to retrieve all email communications from Weller using school equipment over the past six months. The technology manager complied and provided Mr. Parker with hard copies of Weller's email communications from his Yahoo account, his school email account, and his social network account.

Upon review of Weller's school email account, Mr. Parker found nothing contrary to daily school communications. His Yahoo account provided communications between his attorney and himself, and personal emails from friends and family. However, his social networking account provided information about a sexual relationship with another school employee and some other disturbing information.

In more than five different communications, Weller wrote that he wanted to "sand bag" his wife for the "hell she was putting him through." The communications became more intense and detailed Weller's plans to tie sand bags to his wife's feet and release her into deep water in the nearby bay. Mr. Parker consulted with the school's attorney and was advised to contact the police with the information.

Brian Weller was arrested and charged. He was suspended and later dismissed from employment with the school. It was determined that there was enough evidence to try the case and possibly convict Weller, but he decided to waive a trial. Weller received probation before judgment for one year. About a month later, Mr. Parker learned that Weller had filed a lawsuit against him and the school in the amount of $10 million. The lawyers were considering a settlement.

During the courtroom proceedings that followed, the attorneys for the accused contended that the communications presented in pre-case disclosures of evidence motions belonged exclusively to the defendant. The employer had no right to capture, review, or distribute any such cyber records. They cited:

> The Privacy Act of 1974 protects records that can be retrieved by other parties without permission such as a name, social security number, birth date, address, or other identifiable information. The Privacy Act only protects and covers records in the possession and control of federal agencies. An individual is allowed access to his/her records and has permission to request the records if applicable (Services, 2011). The Privacy Act prohibits disclosure of these records without the written consent of the individual to whom the records pertain unless otherwise stated in the Privacy Act.

The attorneys further submitted that the employer had not obtained express written consent from the employee to take into custody said communications.

The prosecution presented the following in a brief as a response to the defense's counter motions:

> The Supreme Court has stated that privacy rights in conjunction with communications do not extend to employees using company-owned computer systems, even in situations where employees have password-protected accounts. Incidents that found employers monitoring their employees' electronic transmissions involving email, Internet, and computer file usage on company owned equipment have not been identified by the court as invasions of privacy.

QUESTIONS

1. Discuss in class your understanding of a privacy policy.

2. Describe your district's policy on privacy statement as it relates to individuals' rights.

3. List the areas of privacy that relate to this case.

4. Write or revise a policy on privacy.

ACTIVITY

1. In small group discussions identify from the list of stakeholders below the individuals that are affected by the dilemma in the vignette and brainstorm ways they can affect change.

2. How do they communicate and in what forum?

3. Discuss your school or district's written plan of action for this problem, if one exists.

4. Identify any resources that could be utilized to resolve this dilemma.

5. Have one person in your group take notes and share your group's findings in front of the class after the discussion.

6. Organize the consensus.

Outside Government Agencies	Outside Technology Professionals
Parents	Crisis Team
Principals	Outside Private Agencies
Staff	School Lawyers
Students	Counselor
Superintendent	School Board
Teachers	Media (TV, Radio, Internet)
Technology Personnel	State's Attorney

Chapter 11

Cyber Risk Assessment Checklist Profile and Questionnaire

The Risk Assessment Checklist and Profile Instrument will give educational leaders a tool to measure the levels of cyber threat through policies governing their organization.

OBJECTIVES
1. List and explain highly restrictive, moderately restrictive or an open environment for protecting sensitive financial and personal data.
2. Explain cyber exposure.
3. Identify and explain briefly the eight best practices policies.

RELATED ELCC STANDARDS
Standard 5.0
Standard 6.0
Standard 7.0

INTRODUCTION

The authors have worked with schools, organizations, and insurance services, across Maryland, Virginia, and Delaware, and have developed a Best Practices Cyber Risk Assessment Profile and Questionnaire which helps agents and brokers manage policies for cyber tangibles and intangibles. Since cyber coverage is an emerging area, agents and brokers need to revisit existing insurance policies to examine the risk of exposure to the potential losses of their client's data.

For educational leaders, the Cyber Risk Assessment Profile and Questionnaire is a methodical walk through an organization's physical and data security policies, which allows a stewardship between school leaders and school districts. This process provides an opportunity for open dialogue to discuss accomplishments, ongoing projects, and new cyber issues. According to many agents and brokers who insure schools, "this process enables risk managers to better address their client's exposures and to effectively utilize the Insurance Services available by development of a Client Service Cyber Plan."

According to Moore's Law (1970), there are significant changes in technologies about every 18 months. Therefore, the Cyber Risk Assessment Profile and Questionnaire allows organizations to proactively deliver innovative and dynamic cyber risk management solutions and thereby reduce exposure. Additionally, this Cyber Risk Assessment Profile and Questionnaire allows risk managers more effective communication with the client's technology personnel. It is no secret that greater portions of organizational assets are increasingly dependent upon the protection of organizational data and customers' data.

A 2006 CNET News article indicates, "The FBI calculated the price tag by extrapolating results from a survey of 2,066 organizations." When examined closely "the survey found that 1,324 respondents, or 64 percent, suffered a financial loss from computer security incidents over a 12-month period." Furthermore, "viruses, spyware, PC thefts and other computer-related crimes cost U.S. business a staggering $67 billion a year, according to the FBI" (Evers, 2006).

While internal and external cyber threats exist in all organizations today, there is a growing need to develop cyber policies that find and identify cyber exposure. This can greatly reduce the risks associated with cyber liability. Cyber exposure can be reduced by understanding an organization's practices and how much weight is placed on data protection.

How does a school or school district examine cyber risks in relationship to cyber exposure? Cyber Risk Assessment Profile and Questionnaire is a tool developed by university researchers. It asks a series of questions in specific areas of network security and physical security while providing risk measurements. For example, does the client's organizational practice require the network to be *highly restrictive* protecting sensitive financial and personal data, *moderately restrictive* protecting customer data, or an *open environment*?

The Cyber Risk Assessment Profile and Questionnaire covers an in-depth examination of an organization's information system, policies, and practices, outlined in earlier chapters. These areas include:

- Security policies
- Acceptable use policies
- Authentication policies (SSL, ciphers, and encryption)
- Internet policies utilizing filters
- Privacy policies
- Access policies
- Auditing policies
- Data protection policies.

Technology risk managers can assist in hardening the organization's infra-structure, providing network administrators with an awareness of security-related issues and the essential skills they need to implement security in their organization's network. Additionally, this will harden defenses against network attacks, strengthen firewalls, secure wireless access points, strengthen network configurations, shore up intrusion detection configurations, monitor encryption, certificates, signatures, and other network security policies.

These best policy practices include all e-business, e-commerce, business, and educational institutions that can only reduce the risk of current cyber threats to their organization's data. It is not a matter of whether an attack or loss will occur. It is a matter of when and how much it will cost an organization.

Cyber Risk Assessment Profile Checklist

Does your organization have a network security policy that includes the following? Circle one of the options. Example: (Yes) No Don't Know

Acceptable use policy

Yes No Don't Know   Employee signed acceptable use policy
Yes No Don't Know   Acceptable use policy (reviewed by attorney)

Authentication policy

Yes No Don't Know   Authentication policy for SSL, ciphers, and encryption
Yes No Don't Know   Site certificate

Internet-use policy

Yes No Don't Know   Internet-use policies utilizing filters
Yes No Don't Know   Download rule
Yes No Don't Know   Explicit materials rule
Yes No Don't Know   Video and media streaming rule
Yes No Don't Know   Pop-ups and advertising rule
Yes No Don't Know   Music rule
Yes No Don't Know   Games rule
Yes No Don't Know   Dating rule
Yes No Don't Know   Email rule
Yes No Don't Know   Other organizational rules

Access policy

Yes No Don't Know   Password and logon requirements and complexities
Yes No Don't Know   Monitoring and auditing network access logons

---

Yes   No   Don't Know   Logon limit hours and locations
Yes   No   Don't Know   Rights and privileges
Yes   No   Don't Know   Two or more open network ports
Yes   No   Don't Know   Unattended idle configuration
Yes   No   Don't Know   Wireless access
Yes   No   Don't Know   Wireless access tools
Yes   No   Don't Know   Remote access
Yes   No   Don't Know   Workstations frozen with Deepfreeze or Clean Slate
Yes   No   Don't Know   Biometrics

Auditing policy

Yes   No   Don't Know   Data protection

Physical policy

Yes   No   Don't Know   Secure physical access to network equipment
Yes   No   Don't Know   Secure network data
Yes   No   Don't Know   Locked individual computers
Yes   No   Don't Know   The prohibition of computers, laptops, notebooks leaving the premises? (Laptops, notebooks)

Analysis policy

Yes   No   Don't Know   TCP packet analysis
Yes   No   Don't Know   OS hardening
Yes   No   Don't Know   Router security
Yes   No   Don't Know   Firewall systems (access control list)
Yes   No   Don't Know   Encryption (IP security)(Point-to-Point Tunneling Protocol)
Yes   No   Don't Know   Network address translation
Yes   No   Don't Know   Intrusion detection/prevention systems
Yes   No   Don't Know   Virus, Malware, Worm, Spyware, Backdoor, spam, and pop-up protection
Yes   No   Don't Know   Disaster recovery plan on or off site

Privacy policy

Yes   No   Don't Know   Privacy statement

Scoring Guide Total 40 pts. Only score "Yes" responses.
(40–31 Low risk, 30–21 Medium risk, 20–11 High risk, 10–0 Very high risk)

Score: _____

Cyber Risk Assessment Questionnaire

Directions: Answer the question to the best of your knowledge.

1. Who is the ISP?

2. Does your organization utilize an intranet or extranet?

3. How many users are there?

4. Does your company have a computer inventory or technology inventory?

5. Are files and folders shared on the network (permissions)?

6. Are there scheduled audits?

7. When and how often does your company back up the system?

8. Are there regular scheduled software and system updates?

9. What percentage of technology does your company outsource? Please list.

CONCLUSION

For educational leaders the Cyber Risk Assessment Profile and Questionnaire is a resource methodology created by university experts and researchers. It is a vital tool for organizations, businesses, and educational institutions for finding risk management solutions and a structured way of safeguarding client's critical electronic assets. The Cyber Risk Assessment Profile and Questionnaire will individualize cyber liability for best policy practices while providing a comprehensive understanding of cyber risk. The next three chapters are considered "Hot Topic" chapters and examine closely such topics as electronic bullying in schools, electronic sexual harassment in schools, and copyright and fair use in schools which should be considered alongside your cyber risk assessment.

QUESTIONS

1. Describe your building/school's analysis policy.

2. Describe your building/school's Internet-use policy.

3. List the areas of concern when writing an Internet-use policy.

4. Write an Internet-use policy.

See the Supplemental for Field Experiences with Assignment and Assessment Rubric on the book's companion website.

Chapter 12

Electronic Bullying

KEY CONCEPTS

Federal government position on electronic bullying
Legislation against electronic bullying
Research on electronic bullying
Best practices to eliminate electronic bullying
Sex texting
Teen cell phone usage
Victimized or victimless?
Unintended consequences
An approach to a solution
Enhance existing policies
Develop educational campaign
Petitioning legislative support

OBJECTIVES

1. Develop an understanding of best practices into electronic bullying.
2. Describe what the law states about electronic bullying.
3. Identify what is and is not sex texting.
4. Describe what the law states about sex texting.
5. Develop a strategy for dealing with sex texting in schools.

RELATED ELCC STANDARDS

Standard 5.0
Standard 6.0

INTRODUCTION

What should educational leaders know about cyber bullying? Traditionally, bullying is defined as repeated aggressive behavior that is an imbalance of power or influence between people. The act of bullying is consistent with physical or verbal abuse directed towards a person. Physical acts will include hitting, pushing, kicking, or throwing objects at the victim. Verbal abuse, however, is consistent with taunting, cursing, name-calling, as well as subtle or indirect actions, such as social isolation and rumor-spreading about the individual(s). To compare the traditional bullying concept with electronic bullying; unlike traditional bullying, perpetrators can remain virtually anonymous using email systems, chat room, instant messaging, and other Internet venues, hiding their identity to avoid personal contact with the victim(s). Raskauskas (2007) mentions that the risk of a real-life bully becoming an electronic bully is quite high and those victims of bullying could turn to electronics to become bullies themselves.

As the proliferations of electronic devices have become available, students have increased their awareness of how to employ the different platforms (e.g. iPad, iPhones, computers, and websites of social networking) for bullying. Students have also expanded their efforts to electronically bully others by using email systems, instant messaging, computer chat room, and/or through digital messages or sending distressing images via the Internet.

The term "electronic bullying" is the use of information and communication technologies to support deliberate, repeated, and hostile behavior by an individual or group that intended to harm others. However, cyber bullying subsequently is when students use the Internet, cell phone, along with other devices to send or post text or images intended to hurt or humiliate others. Electronic bullying isn't limited to students. Typically, adults who are in violation of the electronic state cyber laws are often referred to as cyber-stalking or cyber-harassment, rather than cyber bullying because of the level of punishment and fines imposed on the perpetrators. When the bully or perpetrator uses the Internet to harass others, the Internet-use policy and state's law regarding electronic bullying makes a distinction between perpetrators (minor or adult) to whom the law applies. Electronic bullying has become a serious social issue. It has the potential to cause devastating effects and grief on families and individuals.

FEDERAL GOVERNMENT POSITION ON ELECTRONIC BULLYING

Constitutionally, the federal government has made it illegal to use any electronic device to defame others on the Internet; this means electronic devices cannot be used to coerce intimidate, harass, or cause other substantial emotional distress. Representative Linda Sanchez (D-Calf) and Representative Kenny Hulshof

(R-Mo) proposed a federal law that would criminalize acts of cyber bullying (18 U.S.A. 875c) criminalizes making threats via Internet.

In a recent case, a student was suspended for two days for creating a defamatory video on YouTube.com about another student. Initially, the court ruled in favor of the student, explaining "this court cannot uphold school discipline of student speech simply because young people are unpredictable or immature." The initial ruling was based on the students' right to free speech and expression (First Amendment). However, this ruling was overturned by a higher court, citing that the schools/school district were not able to protect the victim (student) who was harassed. Therefore, the perpetrator could not use the First Amendment (freedom of speech) because the victim (student) did not receive equal protection under the Fourteenth Amendment.

The same court ruled on a similar case one year later, where a student used the Internet to harass two other students in school. The perpetrator sent out an email calling the victims derogatory names and threatening them throughout the email. The court ruled in favor of the school, citing that the schools have the right to discipline students, as long as the school can establish the perpetrator's action disrupted the educational process of the school, or the perpetrator's behavior harmed other members of the student population.

LEGISLATION AGAINST ELECTRONIC BULLYING

Many individual states have established laws or updated legislation regarding electronic bullying to eliminate cyber harassment. Since there are no established federal electronic-bullying laws, these states are changing the language and adding addendums to anti-bullying laws that will address the behaviors of individuals who might abuse Internet privileges. Currently, more than seven states have passed laws against digital harassment. Lawmakers have realized the significance of electronic-bullying issues, and are seeking to establish laws that will deter perpetrators from Internet abuse. Electronic bullying is a new form of bullying that may threaten adolescent social and emotional development (Raskauskas & Stoltz, 2007). Also, there are not currently any specific electronic-bullying laws that address Internet violations. Delaware, New York, Rhode Island, Maryland, and Missouri are actively working at the state level to create current electronic-bullying laws.

RESEARCH ON ELECTRONIC BULLYING

Justin Patchin and Sameer Hinduja (2010), leading authors on cyber bullying, explain that the most powerful preventive step schools can take is to educate the school community about responsible Internet use. Researchers have reported that cyber bullying or electronic-bullying incidents have steadily increased over several years.

Robin M. Kowalski and Susan P. Limber, both from Clemson University, Psychology Department, completed a study published in the *Journal of Adolescent Health* which addressed electronic bullying among middle school students. Kowalski and Limber's study included 3767 students in grades 6, 7 and 8 who attended six elementary and middle schools in the southeastern and northwestern United States and completed a questionnaire. The questionnaire included 23 questions developed for the purpose of their survey. The study examined participants' experience performing electronic-bullying acts or becoming a victim of electronic bullying. According to Kowalski and Limber (2007) findings revealed of the students surveyed, 11 percent of the population had been electronically bullied at least once (victim only). Seven percent of the population surveyed indicated they were bullying victims, and 4 percent of the population surveyed had electronically bullied someone else at least once (bullies only). According to this survey, the most common methods of electronic bullying (reported by both victims and perpetrators) involved the use of instant messaging, chat room, and email systems.

BEST PRACTICES TO ELIMINATE ELECTRONIC BULLYING

Agencies within the federal government including the court system and department of education should assume the responsibility of overseeing the electronic bully policy.

This policy must include a clear definition of what cyber bullying is, and elaborate on the distinction between electronic bullying and face-to-face bullying. Consequences, penalties, and charges must be spelled out in the policy so that parents and students will know what to expect when individuals violate the policy. The department of education should pass down mandates to enforce and oversee the promotion of the policy. In line with the promotion of the policy, the department of education should provide support with prevention and awareness programs to ensure that stakeholders are aware of the consequences. On the other hand, school districts must report all violators, and determine the level of involvement of each case, so that appropriate punishment can be assessed. Sole (2011) stated that the policy should require districts to post the confirmed number of harassment, intimidation, and bullying incidents for each semester, or roughly 18 weeks of school, on its website. One of the most alarming concerns related to electronic bullying is that of sex texting.

SEX TEXTING

Sex texting or "sexting" is a unique phenomenon on a number of levels. The National Center for Missing and Exploited Children identifies sexting as the sharing of nude or seminude images among peers (Nathan, 2009). The following case is an example of a "worst-case" scenario.

Friday afternoon, a 15-year-old high school student forwards a topless picture of herself via cell phone to her boyfriend. The girl is wearing a cheerleader's sweater from her boyfriend's high school. The picture quickly navigates local cyberspace via cell phone, Facebook, and Twitter. Monday morning the principal finds an anonymous envelope slipped under her door. Enclosed is the "topless cheerleader" picture. Recognizing the team logo, the fast-acting controversy-avoiding principal immediately calls in the cheerleading coach who cannot identify the topless girl in the picture. Over the course of the morning, the principal shows the picture to three assistant principals, the dean of discipline, four discipline assistants, three coaches, and four gym teachers in an effort to identify the culprit. One of the gym teachers thinks he has seen the girl hanging out with one of the football players. The football player is called in and identifies the "cheerleader" as his girlfriend. He borrowed the sweater from one of the actual school cheerleaders because he wanted to see his girlfriend in a Playboy-like pose. He saw no harm because he only sent it to a few football teammates. Wanting to avoid suspension, the football player provides contact information of his girlfriend. All coaches are told to alert all players to erase the photo from their cell phones if they received it. The principal alerts local police of the incident. The football player and his girlfriend are arrested for "possession of criminal tools and illegal use of a minor in nudity-oriented materials." Both will be charged with distribution of under-age pornography and he would be registered as a sex offender. The principal is ambushed by a local reporter who received another anonymous envelope containing the topless picture. The reporter edits a news piece that shows an edited version of the topless picture and shows the principal refusing to comment; angrily telling the reporter to contact the school legal counsel. The parents of the young starlet, already in shock after being contacted by the police and informed of the incident, see the report on the evening news and, within 24 hours, the principal and school district are sued by the parents, claiming their daughter's constitutional rights were violated when the principal showed the embarrassing picture to other adults and did not properly report the incident immediately to police as required. The parents want the principal to be arrested and charged with "failure to report child abuse," felony possession of child pornography, and distribution of child pornography. The local TV report is picked up and quickly goes national. The topless girl in the photograph is inundated by social media responses to the story. Distraught over being propositioned online for sex and being labeled a prostitute over various Internet sites, the young girl who sent her boyfriend a "gift" commits suicide, claiming in a suicide note her life has been ruined. The young girl took the picture of herself in the cheerleader sweater eight days prior.

This scenario is actually a combination of three real events that occurred in 2010. The term sexting is so current that a definition of the word cannot be found in the Merriam-Webster Online Dictionary or the Cambridge Dictionaries Online. However the Oxford Dictionaries Online define sexting as "the sending of sexually explicit photographs or messages via mobile phone" (Oxford Dictionaries Online, 2012). Dictionary.com is more detailed in attempting to define the culturally current cyber-activity: "the sending of sexually explicit photos, images, text messages, or emails by using a cell phone or other mobile device" (Dictionary.com, 2012). It is no wonder that principals, teachers, and administrators born in the 1950s and 1960s are not only shocked by the act of student sexting but are also immobilized by the realization that young people could be so proficient at utilizing a technology that many older people don't understand. How can a typical educational administrator prepare for a technology they barely comprehend? In this situation, the optimal answer is to educate the educator with current information, current experiences, and best practices.

TEEN CELL PHONE USAGE

For the modern teen (ages 12 to 17), according to Pew (Lenhart, 2009) cell phones have become the preferred method of communication, social integration, and mode of learning about the world at large. Processes that used to depend on verbal communication and face-to-face contact are today digitized and transmitted. In 2010, the Pew Internet and American Life Project reported that 75 percent of all teens own cell phones and 88 percent of those owners are texting. On any given day, 33 percent of teens communicate with friends face to face, 11 percent via email, 38 percent by cell phone, and 25 percent through social network sites, but the favorite is text messaging commanding 54 percent of all teen communication (Lenhart, 2009).

Perhaps what is most appealing to teens is that text messaging solves the inconvenience of silence in the classroom. Where most forms of teen communication require access to vocal chords or computers, cell phone texting can be accomplished with stealth and ease. Using a cell phone that is the size of a credit card and can easily be cupped in the palm of the hand, a student suffering through a boring physics class can easily communicate with their best friend across town using only one finger to type a message. Most teens can effectively live a texting life with no more than 3rd grade writing abilities.

The advent of the cell phone as a miniaturized multimedia computer is a benefit often lost on older technology-confused adults but embraced by technology-savvy teens. The Pew Internet and American Life Project found that 83 percent of all teen cell phone users use their phones to take pictures, 64 percent share cell phone pictures with others, and 32 percent exchange videos on their cell phones (Pew Research, 2010). Considering these statistics, for the average teen exploring their sexuality, is the evolvement of teen sexting any wonder?

Sexting is a unique phenomenon on a number of levels. The National Center for Missing and Exploited Children identifies sexting as the sharing of nude or seminude images among peers (IP Law Blog, 2009). The National Center for the Prosecution of Child Abuse, characterizes the process of sexting as "self-produced child pornography" (Leary, 2008). Sexting does not qualify as harmful or inappropriate speech disseminated through school or district communication systems thereby hampering a school's authority to regulate or even investigate, so how are school officials to protect the common good? In the paragraphs to follow, we provide some best practices for school leaders.

VICTIMIZED OR VICTIMLESS?

Some technologists may argue sexting is not a victimless crime. In the adult world, sending a picture between boyfriend and girlfriend may be deemed as permissible interpersonal activity. However, forwarding that same picture to other parties without the expressed knowledge or consent of the original party is a crime against the original sender. In the case of sexting among teens, the sender is digitally transmitting a pornographic image of an under-aged individual and thereby breaking laws applicable to pedophiles. Similar to the issues surrounding cyber bullying, combating sexting requires presenting challenging interpretations of the law in order to maintain the integrity of freedom of speech rights (Willard, 2010).

A 2009 Pew survey of teens and sexting found:

- 4% of cell-owning teens have sent sexually suggestive nude or nearly nude images of themselves to someone via cell phone.
- 15% of cell-owning teens have received sexually suggestive nude or nearly nude images of someone they knew via cell phone.
- Older teens and teens that pay their own telephone bills are more likely to send or receive "sexts".
- Focus groups revealed that most sexting occurs between 1) two romantic partners, 2) partners that have exchanged with others, and 3) people seeking to be in a relationship with the exchanger.

(Lenhart, 2009, p. 1)

A 2009 incident in Pennsylvania points out the intricacies of defining, identifying, and applying/enforcing regulations to incidences of sexting. A local district attorney threatened to charge 17 teens identified in sexted images with child pornography unless they agreed to probation and an afterschool program (Lenhart, 2009). The program would include six to nine months of classes in which participants would have to address issues of self-concept, sexual violence, and harassment (Taylor, 2010). Representing three of the families, the American Civil Liberties Union sued the district attorney claiming two of the girls should not be held responsible since they did not give permission to have their images distributed (Lenhart, 2009). Furthermore, the courts agreed that the district attorney violated the parents' Fourteenth Amendment rights to due process in the upbringing of their children and also violated the First Amendment rights of the teens to appear in the photographs in question (Taylor, 2010).

UNINTENDED CONSEQUENCES

In addition to treading into undefined waters, the average school administrator needs to consider the unintended consequences of applying poorly defined statutes to the issue of sexting. First, following through with current laws will brand the offending teen as a sex offender, requiring the teen's name to be entered into the sex offender registry. The registry does not distinguish between pedophiles, rapists, or sexters and the information is publicly assessable. The long-term effect of the sex offender registry is to cut the offender off from society (Ostrager, 2010). Second, including young people in the sex offender registry for sexting offenses will overload the system and minimize the original intent of the registry. Currently over 674,000 U.S. citizens are listed in the registry with hundreds more being added every week. The ability of the police to monitor dangerous sex offenders is waning (Ostrager, 2010). Finally, medical science and the court system agree the differences between the under-developed adolescent brain and the mature brain are considerable enough to warrant a two-tier judicial system. Criminalizing teens for sexting is an inappropriate response to meeting the emotional needs of the offender and could be creating more problems than intended (Ostrager, 2010).

AN APPROACH TO A SOLUTION

As academic administrators move beyond the surprise and shock factor, the question remains, what procedures should academic leaders apply to deal with and prevent sexting? A threefold process should be initiated to protect students, adults, and the school/district.

Step one: enhance policies to manage and address the problem.
Step two: develop a campaign/education plan to combat sexting and cyber bullying.
Step three: get involved in petitioning legislators for policy changes.

ENHANCE EXISTING POLICIES

Policy changes to address sexting should pay close attention to complying with and maintaining Fourth Amendment rights.

1. School policies should explicitly prohibit sexting. Policy changes should clearly state that if a school administrator has a reasonable reason to believe a sexting policy has been violated, search and seizure of cell phones is possible.
2. School administrators must ask permission to search a student's cell phone. If permission is not granted, school administrators must alert the student's parents of the suspected sexting situation.
3. If sexting evidence is found, the electronic device should be placed in an envelope and sealed for investigation by police.
4. Administrator is to contact the parents of all students involved in a sexting incident.
5. Contact police and alert authorities of the sexting incident.
6. Report the sexting incident to local and state authorities under the rules of reporting child abuse or neglect.
7. Discipline the students involved in the transmission according to policy being careful to identify and protect students that have been victimized.

(Long & Caradine, 2010, p.23)

DEVELOP EDUCATIONAL CAMPAIGN

1. Vice-principals, disciplinarians, counselors, prevention resource officers and instructors should be trained to identify instances of sexting, trained in procedures to maintain student rights, and to contact immediate supervisors.
2. Students are to be made aware in print and via instruction of the changes in policy. Students are to participate in educational sessions by qualified instructors to identify and protect against instances and situations that can lead to sexting.
3. Students are to be instructed in appropriate procedures to report situations in which they feel they have been victimized by a sexting situation.
4. Students should receive instruction in dealing with issues of self-concept, sexual violence, and harassment.
5. The school should prepare to provide instruction to parents and community similar to instruction provided to counselors and students.

6. Set up a hotline for parents and students to report instances of sexting.

(Wong-Lo & Bullock, 2011, pp. 64–70)

PETITIONING LEGISLATIVE SUPPORT

1. Principal should consult with school district for permission to become proactive in supporting anti-sexting legislation.
2. If legislation is not current, the principal should investigate steps needed to form a community coalition of students, parents and business to petition local legislators.
3. If legislation is current, the principal should create activities to show school & district support for passage of legislation.

(Long & Caradine, 2010, p. 23)

CONCLUSION

As research on sexting and its causes, motives, and outcomes continue to develop, policies and best practices for educational administrators will be disseminated on a wide basis. As technology grows and changes, it is unlikely that incidences of sexting and cyber bullying will disappear. The problem is more likely to morph into a different form or technology. The best policy is to develop a policy that is flexible and changeable but keeps the rights and protection of victimized students and parents as a central focus. Inaction and ignorance will have the most damaging effect as technology continues to advance. An administrative culture built on the awareness of social media norms and how young people use technology is perhaps the best defense against the damages that could be inflicted as a result of such evolving issues. Next, we will examine electronic sexual harassment.

QUESTIONS

1. Describe three things that students should not do on the Internet.

2. List ten ways to end electronic bullying in your school.

3. Develop an awareness/prevention program outline.

4. Develop a possible electronic-bullying campaign using signs, slogans, and posters.

VIGNETTE CHAPTER 12   Did I Do Something Wrong?

Norman G. Holiday High School is located just off the East Atlantic coast and has suffered hard economic times in the past 10 years. Each year the administrators are asked to run the school with lesser and lesser funding. Mr. Randolph has been a high school teacher for 10 years and assistant principal for another 8 years. He is considered a transformational leader who deals well with a changing school environment.

Mr. Kipling has been a high school science teacher for 17 years. He has good observation reports and excellent evaluations from the administration. Patrick Phillips is a freshman in Mr. Kipling's science class.

David Phillips, Patrick's father, was going through his son's social network site and discovered a disturbing photograph. The photo showed his son standing against a blackboard with his nose pressed against it. He called his son to the kitchen and questioned him about the photo.

Patrick explained that Mr. Kipling gives students a choice when they break one of his rules or say something inappropriate. A student can choose to accept a referral to the principal's office. Or the student can choose to pay a quarter and put it in a jar that Mr. Kipling keeps in a drawer. If the student is unable to pay, he can choose to stand with his nose pressed against the blackboard for two minutes while the class makes fun of him. Students take photos with cell phones and post them on the Internet so other students can make fun of the student. Patrick explained that most students choose to pay the quarter. He then showed his father over 30 photos of his class mates with their noses against the blackboard. Patrick said that Mr. Kipling bragged that he had collected well over $100 in one semester, but he didn't know what Mr. Kipling did with the money.

The next day Mr. Phillips made an appointment with the assistant principal, Mr. Randolph. During the meeting Mr. Phillips explained what he discovered and shared his son's story. He also provided printouts of several children in the classroom with their noses against the blackboard. Mr. Randolph said he would investigate the concerns and would get back to Mr. Phillips with some answers.

Mr. Randolph called Mr. Kipling to the office and questioned him about his disciplinary methods. Mr. Kipling admitted that he gave students choices for cursing, acting out, or disrupting class. He shared that he had been using this method since the beginning of the school year. Mr. Kipling added that other teachers were giving students similar choices so that they could avoid referrals to the principal's office. Some teachers were having students do pushups, and other teachers had students do extra assignments or pay money to avoid referrals. "It's no different than making them stay after school to clean the classroom or chalk boards," Mr. Kipling said.

When asked about the money he collected from students, Mr. Kipling responded:

> At the beginning of the year, you stated there were way too many office referrals last year for things teachers could have handled. You encouraged teachers to find alternative ways of dealing with student's misbehavior because you wanted a dramatic decrease in the number of referrals. You also said that supplies for teachers were extremely limited because of budget cuts. So teachers found creative

101

ways to fundraise and supplement the shortage. I purchase needed supplies for my science class with the money collected and reduced my office referrals to almost zero. I thought that's what you wanted. Did I do something wrong?

QUESTIONS

1. Describe and compare your school policies on referrals.

2. Describe and compare your school policies on cell phone use.

3. Discuss social networking sites and school involvement.

4. Role play reporting this case to the police, to social services, and to the superintendent.

5. Write a policy on fundraisers.

ACTIVITY

1. In small group discussions identify from the list of stakeholders below the individuals that are affected by the dilemma in the vignette and brainstorm ways they can affect change.

2. How do they communicate and in what forum?

3. Discuss your school or district's written plan of action for this problem, if one exists.

4. Identify any resources that could be utilized to resolve this dilemma.

5. Have one person in your group take notes and share your group's findings in front of the class after the discussion.

6. Organize the consensus.

Outside Government Agencies	Outside Technology Professionals
Parents	Crisis Team
Principals	Outside Private Agencies
Staff	School Lawyers
Students	Counselor
Superintendent	School Board
Teachers	Media (TV, Radio, Internet)
Technology Personnel	State's Attorney

Chapter 13

Electronic Sexual Harassment

KEY CONCEPTS
Impact of cyber bullying
Electronic sexual harassment increasing dramatically
Freedom of speech
Electronic sexual harassment and the law
Technologies
Theories of sexual harassment
Sexual harassment is a growing problem
Changing the school culture and climate

OBJECTIVES
1. Define electronic sexual harassment and the law.
2. List the components of sexual harassment.
3. Explain the legal aspects of electronic sexual harassment.

RELATED ELCC STANDARDS
Standard 5.0
Standard 6.0

INTRODUCTION

Educational technology promises to transform the classroom experience for students, teachers, and parents. Educational leaders most take note of innovations in educational technology, especially Internet-based innovations, that are occurring so rapidly that statutory and case law are continually developing and struggling to keep pace with them (Quinn, 2003). Implications for school leaders are directed to change in this time of technology. Immersed in their complex daily lives, leaders can find it nearly impossible to keep up with the swiftly moving legal landscape in educational technology (Quinn, 2003). Researchers state that the laws have not kept up with the Internet explosion. For this reason, schools must take existing law and try to figure out where a court may rule (Quinn, 2003). They must evaluate the existing law and then predict how the courts will go forward with these issues in an Internet case. With this in mind, the school law researcher and administrator's role should be to communicate frequently with educators about new statutes and how to apply legal concepts and frameworks to these developing situations (Quinn, 2003).

Researchers have explored the reporting practices of bullying to school officials and other adults, and have provided insight into the growing problem of cyber bullying to help inform educators and policymakers of the appropriate prevention or intervention measures to counter cyber bullying (Cassidy, Jackson, & Brown, 2009). Educators and the public are often perplexed by the enormous and evolving cyber harassment and bullying occurrences. Youth of the digital generation are interacting in ways our fore-mothers and fathers never imagined; using electronic communications that until 30 years ago never existed (Cassidy, Jackson, & Brown, 2009).

IMPACT OF CYBER BULLYING

The extent and impact of cyber bullying, such as harassment, labeling (gay, lesbian), negative language, sexual connotations, and solicitation, is upsetting to school culture. Harassment covers a wide range of behaviors of an offensive nature. It is commonly understood as behavior intended to disturb or upset, and it is characteristically repetitive (Harassment, 2012). In the legal sense, it is intentional behavior that is found threatening or disturbing. Sexual harassment refers to persistent and unwanted sexual advances, typically in the workplace, where the consequences of refusing are potentially very disadvantageous to the victim (Sexual harassment, 2012). Sexual harassment has been around for decades but, within the past 5 years, sexual harassment has advanced into electronic sexual harassment. Electronic sexual harassment is a term referring to the use of electronic devices to harass, torture, or physically harm a person in a sexual manner (Electronic sexual harassment, 2012). Researchers state that with the advent of social networks, weblogs, and chat rooms, emails have somehow become practically obsolete. The only purpose they now serve, it seems, is when one party has to send a formal letter to another party or to multiple recipients. Emails are now all about business. Recently computers, cell phones, iPads, emails, and social networks have been used for employee abuse and electronic sexual harassment, specifically administrators vs. teachers and teachers vs. students within schools.

In truth, employees have been abusing various electronic communications: computers, cell phones, iPads, emails, and social networks, and the number of cases has increased over the years (Jansen, 2012). These are cases proven by small and big companies alike. For instance, Dow Chemical Company fired 39 employees and disciplined 200 in 2000 due to email abuse (Jansen, 2012). It was not simply the use of emails but how they were used—they included off-color jokes and pornography (pictures of naked women and depiction of sex acts) (Jansen, 2012). Similar cases happened in other companies: The *New York Times* (1999)—23 employees sent obscene emails, Xerox (1999)—40 employees used the Internet "inappropriately," Compaq (2001)—20 employees logged on to porn sites, and all of these employees were fired (Jansen, 2012).

ELECTRONIC SEXUAL HARASSMENT INCREASING DRAMATICALLY

Just as electronic sexual harassment has increased dramatically within different companies, it has also increased in the public school system between administrators and teachers, and teachers and students. During the past decade and a half, researchers have made the field of educational administration a focal point due to the considerable support exemplary school principals have given teachers in schools where electronic sexual harassment has taken place (Blase & Blase, 2002). Many teachers have complained of being subjected to long-term mistreatment from their school principal. Electronic sexual harassment can have psychological/ emotional effects, physical/physiological effects, and have effects on classroom instruction and relationships with the students (Blase & Blase, 2002). Researchers state that effective principal leadership can have important effects on student learning (Blase & Blase, 2002). The principals, who are supposed to develop positive relationships based on mutual trust, respect, openness, support, and understanding, cannot become effective if they are contributing to electronic sexual harassment. It is not acceptable for a teacher to be in a workplace that tolerates such behavior. As electronic sexual harassment also comes in graphic versions, receiving such emails from your administrator, principal, bosses, or colleagues, is offensive, however unintentional it is (Jansen, 2012). It would be even more offensive to find out that the message that was sent from the computer, cell phone, iPad, email account, or social network account, in whatever form, has been sent to millions of other people. That is a form of electronic sexual harassment.

New technologies have the potential to revolutionize the educational system. Repercussions for school leaders are significant and include technology-related issues involving freedom of speech, harassment, and privacy. School leaders need to be mindful of these emerging legal conditions and understand the importance of professional development training for educators in technology and the law (Quinn, 2003).

Since electronic sexual harassment involves behavior of an offensive nature involving computers, cell phones, iPads, emails, and social networks, many laws have come into question with cases involving electronic sexual harassment. According to Quinn (2003) with reference to the First Amendment, Congress shall make no law respecting an establishment of religion, or prohibiting the free exercise thereof; abridging the freedom of speech or of the press; or the right of the people peaceably to assemble and to petition the government for a redress of grievances.

FREEDOM OF SPEECH

Another free speech development is the emergence of court cases involving student-developed websites that include derogatory and even threatening statements and images about students, teachers, administrators, and/or the school itself (Quinn, 2003). Title VII of the Civil Rights Act of 1964 includes provisions in which verbal or written conduct that has the effect of interfering with an individual's work performance or of creating an intimidating, hostile, or offensive work environment may constitute a civil rights violation if the behavior is so severe or insidious that it alters an employee's working condition (Quinn, 2003). As a result, a school district may be held legally responsible for a hostile environment created by a supervisor with authority over an employee (Quinn, 2003). If harassing conduct by a supervisor, administrator, or teacher is present, the only way to avoid liability is to demonstrate that the school district employed reasonable attention to avoid the harassment and that the employee unreasonably failed to avail him/herself of the school's reporting procedure.

ELECTRONIC SEXUAL HARASSMENT AND THE LAW

The Family Educational Rights and Privacy Act of 1974 established the following four areas of concern regarding student privacy: (1) student information that is placed on the district website or otherwise distributed through the Internet by school staff members or other students, (2) disclosure of confidential student information by staff members through electronic communications, (3) information that students disclose about themselves in email messages or on various websites, and (4) school-corporate partnerships that provide the opportunity for companies to gather or solicit personal information from students (Quinn, 2003).

The Supreme Court applied the Temporary Lifting Order (TLO) standards of whether a search was justified and reasonable. The court held that employees had constitutionally protected privacy interests in the work environment. The rationality of the expectation of privacy must be determined on a case-by-case basis. Electronic communications of public employees are typically considered to be discoverable under public record laws. It could therefore be argued that employees have no expectation of privacy. However, common practice is to treat email as private, which would lead to the reasonable expectation that unless there is a public records request, the privacy of employees' email will be honored (Quinn, 2003).

TECHNOLOGIES

Technology raises many challenging issues for school leaders. To avoid litigation, administrators must become knowledgeable about at least the fundamentals of technology-related school law. A recent movement to address this and other technology-related concerns is the creation and adoption of national technology standards for school leaders (Quinn, 2003).

We are at the beginning of a revolution in educational technology that will transform the way we look at learning and teaching (Quinn, 2003). The potential benefits of these innovations are inspiring for students, educators, administrators, and parents. According to Agger and Day (2011) this transformation does not, however, come free of problems. As with any advance, there is always the prospect of misuse and abuse of new technologies. Legal issues pertinent to this modernization include the First Amendment, harassment, privacy, and Title IX for legal protection (Agger and Day 2011). School leaders must be well informed in such matters to minimize the distractions and liabilities and to maximize the learning potential afforded by educational technology now that three-fourths of students are reporting these incidences.

Sexual harassment is an issue that has been around since the early 1970s after women started to assert their independence and enter themselves in the workforce. However, sexual harassment has moved from the boardroom to the classroom and has become a growing epidemic among young adolescents. It is reported by the American Association of University Women (AAUW) (Hill & Kearl, 2011) that 80 percent of secondary students have experienced some sort of sexually based harassment. While most of these behaviors are directed by students towards students, they can be directed by students towards teachers and vice versa. Sexual harassment can occur anywhere and anytime in public schools, however things can be changed by being proactive. The first step in being proactive is to isolate the causes of sexual harassment.

THEORIES OF SEXUAL HARASSMENT

According to Lee, Croninger, Linn, and Chen (1996) there are several theories on why sexual harassment occurs. The first theory is biological. As the physical differences become more apparent between the genders and hormones increase, males become more aggressive than females. This hormonally charged aggression can be directed sexually, ultimately meaning that males will become more sexually aggressive towards females. The second theory is development. Human beings learn to communicate through social interactions. However, inappropriate communications or an inability to communicate can lead to sexual harassment. Another theory why sexual harassment occurs is pathology. Simply put, extreme trauma can turn a victim into an aggressor thus creating a vicious cycle. Another theory on why sexual harassment occurs is the abuse of power theory. In this theory, the more power an individual obtains, the more likely they are to abuse it. This theory also views sexual harassment as a way to express dominance, especially when power and authority are threatened in an organization. The media can also be a factor in sexual harassment. Young adolescents often learn social norms and behaviors from television, the Internet, and other forms of mass media. These influences can confuse young adults into thinking that sexual harassment is actually a form of flirting (Young & Ashbaker, 2008). No matter the cause of sexual harassment, the results are the same.

The majority of sexual harassment victims are females. As reported, 80 percent of females and 60 percent of males say they have experienced some sort of sexual harassment while in school (Fogarty, 2009). Students are not the only ones experiencing this. Teachers, while they often do not report it as much as students, are also harassed by students. Thirty-six percent of high school students report that other students sexually harass school faculty and staff. They also report that female staff and faculty are more targeted than males (Shane, 2009).

The means of harassment also varies depending on the gender of the victim. Females tend to receive more unwanted touching and advancements from males and also tend to be victims of inappropriate sexually based jokes. Males, however, tend to experience accusations from their peers about their sexual orientation. The effects that sexual harassment can have on a person can be tremendous, and can torture a victim to the point of withdrawing from school and activities. Approximately, 40 percent of harassment victims respond to their situation through absenteeism (Fogarty, 2009). Harassed students would rather avoid the situation than continue to be harassed. Sexual harassment can also decrease academic performance and students' ability to work. These situations can also help develop hostile environments (Fogarty, 2009). Sexual harassment can also contribute to trouble in sleeping, avoidance of school, or altering schedule or how students get home so they can avoid abusers. Sexual harassment can also create a vicious cycle when the victim expresses their dominance (Hill & Kearl, 2011). These effects can be displayed by victims of any age, including both staff and students.

SEXUAL HARASSMENT IS A GROWING PROBLEM

Although sexual harassment is a growing problem in schools (Young & Ashbaker, 2008), there are things that can be done to reduce the impacts of sexual harassment. One of the most effective means to reduce harassment in schools is to have a clearly written policy that identifies the different types of harassment. However, this policy is only as good as its implementation (Young & Ashbaker, 2008). According to Title IX of the Civil Rights Act, all schools have to have a policy on sexual harassment (Lee, Croninger, Linn, & Chen, 1996). To make sure that these established sexual harassment policies as mandated by Title IX are implemented into schools, it is advised by Maine's Governor's Children Cabinet (2006) that school systems survey and assess the current practices in the schools. This will allow the system to see whether or not changes need to be made to existing policies. This assessment can be done by administering a school climate survey or a needs assessment (Whitted & Dupper, 2005). Periodic assessment should be done with the same chosen instrument in order to assess growth and further development. Once this assessment has been completed, a stakeholder's committee should be established with representatives from the school (i.e. teachers, students, support staff, and administration) as well as the community. This committee should represent the diversity in the community and in the school and meet monthly to discuss the progress of the plan. The responsibility of this committee is to develop school and district rules that address and prevent harassment. This committee is also responsible for advertising these rules to all stakeholders and for initiating and developing professional development opportunities for teachers so they can properly monitor student behavior. Throughout this process the committee will be responsible for evaluating the progress and effectiveness of the new policies (Maine's Governor's Children's Cabinet, 2006). Simply changing school and district policy regarding harassment and establishing a committee will not alleviate the problems associated with sexual harassment.

CHANGING THE SCHOOL CULTURE AND CLIMATE

Whitted and Dupper (2005) suggest an overall change of the school culture and climate. In Whitted and Dupper's design, they suggest implementing programs directed towards bullies, victims, bystanders, families, and community members. The methods they suggest are through intervention and classroom instruction and should replace the old ideas of conflict resolution, peer mediation, and group therapy as a means of stopping harassment. However, these methods might not be effective if the person harassing the student is a teacher or a school-based official.

Today's news reports seem to be filled with stories and allegations of inappropriate relationships and conduct between teachers and students, however there are few reports of harassment. Teacher-student harassment can come in a variety of forms. The first type of sexual harassment used by people in authority is *quid pro quo*. In this form, something is promised by the authority figure in exchange for a sexual act. This can be a higher grade, letter of recommendation, etc. These actions can also be negative, like a reduction in a grade or some other form of blackmail. If the victim wants to avoid or gain the outcome then they will complete the demanded act. Another form of harassment that can be used by authority figures is called the hostile environment. In hostile environments sexual comments, touching, or other inappropriate means interfere with a student's work. Hostile environments can make victims feel unsafe in school (Equal Rights Advocates, 2012). However, many students often do not report these actions. Only 12 percent of students report being harassed by teachers (Brackett & Brackett, 2012). Two factors can be involved in this statistic. One factor is that sexual harassment from teachers only occurs occasionally in the K-12 grades, the other is that harassment is simply not being reported. Unfortunately, if the latter is true and these actions are not being reported, then schools are not liable. This is an issue that is constantly up for review by the U.S. Justice System.

One such case was *Gebser v. Lago Vista Independent School District (1998)*. In this case, a 14-year-old girl was sexually harassed and eventually entered a sexual relationship with one of her teachers. The girl sued the school district, however the U.S. Supreme Court deemed that since the girl did not report the harassment to school officials the school was not liable for the harassment and the rape (Shane, 2009). Proving that authorities are aware inappropriate contact has taken place is very difficult, but it makes school systems and school officials very vulnerable to allegations. This is why all valid allegations should be investigated once they are reported. However, not all officials should be given the responsibility of investigating sexual harassment claims. In fact, under the Code of Federal Regulations it is mandated that each district employ a Title IX coordinator to research and address all issues surrounding gender equality in the district. This person, as well as other persons designated, is also responsible for investigating allegations about sexual harassment and educating staff and volunteers about appropriate conduct (Fetter-Harrott, 2010). Having someone responsible for staff conduct can make a great difference in changing the culture and the climate of the school. However, this accountability is only as effective as the individual in charge.

CONCLUSION

Sexual harassment was once a phenomenon prevalent at the beginning of women's liberation into the workforce. However, sexual harassment is now a growing entity in today's schools and is increasing with the rise of technology. All hope is not lost though. Through active involvement by educational leaders, faculty/staff, and students sexual harassment can be eliminated in schools. However, eliminating this problem is a team effort, one that can only be accomplished with clearly written policies and rules that everyone has to follow no matter their authority or status. Now let's examine our last chapter in this book and close it with the basics of copyright and fair use.

QUESTIONS

1. What is electronic sexual harassment?

2. How does electronic sexual harassment differ from other forms of harassment?

3. Could someone be committing electronic sexual harassment and not know it?

VIGNETTE CHAPTER 13   I Was Only Trying To Help

Rose Crest High School for Girls is a college preparatory school in the northeast. The school is 50 years old and has a tradition of excellence, high student achievement, and college acceptance. Over 95 percent of the students enter a four-year college or university.

Ms. Carol Weber, principal of Rose Crest High School for Girls, is an instructional leader with many intrapersonal skills. She has been the principal for the past 7 years. Mr. Paul Butler has been a teacher of Technology at the school for 12 years. He has an excellent teaching record and one state championship win as coach of Girls' Softball.

One May afternoon, two detectives entered Rose Crest High School for Girls and requested a meeting with Ms. Weber. They explained that they were investigating a parent complaint of unwarranted contact with a minor child who attends Rose Crest High School. The parents reported that their daughter had been exchanging emails and chatting frequently online with a male teacher over the course of several months. The student had also been using her cell phone to contact the teacher. The police obtained an arrest warrant for Paul Butler and were charging him with sexual harassment of a minor and phone misuse or use of an electronic device to commit a crime.

Ms. Weber was shocked at what they were telling her and said, "In the history of this school, there have never been any incidents like the one you are alleging happened." Ms. Weber called Mr. Butler to the office, and the two detectives arrested him as he entered the office. He was handcuffed and escorted to their unmarked police vehicle.

Ms. Weber immediately called the school's headmaster or superintendent. They agreed to suspend Mr. Butler pending the outcome of the case. Mr. Butler was released the next day on $10,000 unsecured bond as he was not considered a risk.

The next day Mr. Butler agreed to a three-way phone conference with the headmaster and Ms. Weber to explain his side of the story. Butler said:

> I've been a teacher at Rose Crest High School for Girls for the past 12 years. I'm married and have two daughters. I'm popular with students and have positive relationships with them. I am the softball coach and class advisor for the 11th grade. I grew up here and know many families. I keep in touch with everyone through social networking where I follow my past students as they make their way through life with college, jobs, and married life. I recently became friends on my social network with several 11th grade girls in my class. There is no school policy about being friends with students outside of school on social networks. As time passed, the girl and I emailed and sometimes chatted with instant messaging. At first we only exchanged chats from home, but as time progressed, I found myself chatting during class and throughout the day. My phone records will show that. We both use smartphones to stay connected. Again, at first the conversations were simple. Then she started asking me about my personal life. I told her that my personal life was private, but she insisted. The conversations turned somewhat friendlier. She told me about her present sexual experience and asked my advice. I was only trying to help her with answers to problems that she couldn't take to her parents. I guess we discussed some things we shouldn't have.

Ms. Weber suspended Mr. Butler without pay pending the outcome of the trial, which would determine his employment with Rose Crest High School.

QUESTIONS

1. Describe your school's policy on social networking with students.

2. Describe your school's policy on phone use with students.

3. Discuss social networking sites and school involvement with sports, band, clubs, and advance placement (AP) courses.

4. Write a policy addressing teachers and students with regard to social networking sites.

ACTIVITY

1. In small group discussions identify from the list of stakeholders below the individuals that are affected by the dilemma in the vignette and brainstorm ways they can affect change.

2. How do they communicate and in what forum?

3. Discuss your school or district's written plan of action for this problem, if one exists.

4. Identify any resources that could be utilized to resolve this dilemma.

5. Have one person in your group take notes and share your group's findings in front of the class after the discussion.

6. Organize the consensus.

Outside Government Agencies	Outside Technology Professionals
Parents	Crisis Team
Principals	Outside Private Agencies
Staff	School Lawyers
Students	Counselor
Superintendent	School Board
Teachers	Media (TV, Radio, Internet)
Technology Personnel	State's Attorney

Chapter 14

Basics of Copyright and Fair Use

KEY CONCEPTS
How copyright is secured
Second-hand sales
Public domain and fair use
Website domain
Copyright lawsuits
Pivotal software licensing lawsuit

OBJECTIVES
1. Develop an understanding of copyright and fair use
2. Examine the legal aspects of copyright.
3. Examine the legal aspects of fair use.

RELATED ELCC STANDARDS
Standard 5.0
Standard 6.0

INTRODUCTION

Understanding copyright, public domain, and fair use helps educational leaders in developing policies to avoid violations of state and federal laws. This chapter explores details of these laws.

Copyright law in the United States is based on the Copyright Act of 1976, a federal statute that went into effect on January 1, 1978 (Radcliffe & Brinson, 1999). The Copyright Act prevents the unauthorized copying of a work of authorship. Copyright is a form of protection provided by the laws of the United States (title 17, U.S. Code) to the authors of "original works of authorship," including literary, dramatic, musical, artistic, and certain other intellectual works. This protection is available to both published and unpublished works. Section 106 of the 1976 Copyright Act generally gives the owner of copyright the exclusive right to do and to authorize others to do the following:

- To reproduce the work in copies or phonorecords.
- To prepare derivative works based upon the work.
- To distribute copies or phonorecords of the work to the public by sale or other transfer of ownership, or by rental, lease, or lending.
- To perform the work publicly, in the case of literary, musical, dramatic, and choreographic works, pantomimes, and motion pictures and other audiovisual works.
- To display the work publicly, in the case of literary, musical, dramatic, and choreographic works, pantomimes, and pictorial, graphic, or sculptural works, including the individual images of a motion picture or other audiovisual work.
- In the case of sound recordings, to perform the work publicly by means of a digital audio transmission. Sound recordings are defined in the law as "works that result from the fixation of a series of musical, spoken, or other sounds, but not including the sounds accompanying a motion picture or other audiovisual work."

HOW COPYRIGHT IS SECURED

The way in which copyright protection is secured is frequently misunderstood. No publication or registration or other action in the Copyright Office is required to secure copyright. Copyright is secured automatically when the work is created, and a work is "created" when it is fixed in copy or phonorecord for the first time. "Copies" are material objects from which a work can be read or visually perceived either directly or with the aid of a machine or device, such as books, manuscripts, sheet music, film, videotape, or microfilm. "Phonorecords" are material objects embodying fixations of sounds (excluding, by statutory definition, motion picture soundtracks), such as cassette tapes, CDs, or vinyl disks. It is up to the author to register their work (U.S. Copyright Office, 2008). Registration is voluntary but recommended, especially if you wish to bring a lawsuit for infringement. In general, copyright registration is a legal formality intended to make a public record of the basic facts of a particular copyright. However, registration is not a condition of copyright protection. Even though registration is not a requirement for protection, the copyright law provides several inducements or advantages to encourage copyright owners to make registration. Among these advantages are the following:

- Registration establishes a public record of the copyright claim.
- Before an infringement suit may be filed in court, registration is necessary for works of U.S. origin.
- If made before or within five years of publication, registration will establish prima facie evidence in court of the validity of the copyright and of the facts stated in the certificate.
- If registration is made within three months after publication of the work or prior to an infringement of the work, statutory damages and attorney's fees will be available to the copyright owner in court actions. Otherwise, only an award of actual damages and profits is available to the copyright owner.
- Registration allows the owner of the copyright to record the registration with the U.S. Customs Service for protection against the importation of infringing copies. Registration may be made at any time within the life of the copyright. Unlike the law before 1978, when a work has been registered in unpublished form, it is not necessary to make another registration when the work becomes published, although the copyright owner may register the published edition, if desired.

(U.S. Copyright Office, 2008)

SECOND-HAND SALES

Does an author get royalties for books that are resold? The answer to this question to some doesn't seem fair. At this point the author does not receive royalties on books that are sold at second-hand book stores. There is a movement that has started to require second-hand (or "used") book stores to pay royalties on books that they resell. Novelists, Inc. a group which claims to be "the international organization of multi-published novelists" is advocating to amend the United States Copyright Law to require that used book stores pay royalties on books they resell for up to two years after their publication. Under the first sale doctrine (section 109 of the Copyright Act), ownership of a physical copy of a copyright-protected work permits lending, reselling, disposing, etc. of the item, but it does not permit reproducing the material, publicly displaying or performing it, or otherwise engaging in any of the acts reserved for the copyright holder, because the transfer of the physical copy does not include transfer of the copyright rights to the work (Copyright Clearance Center, 2012).

PUBLIC DOMAIN AND FAIR USE

How can understanding public domain and fair use help administrators, teachers, and students prevent copyright infringements? To understand what public domain and fair use are, you need to understand copyright on published work. Copyright is a form of protection provided by the laws of the United States (title 17, U.S. Code) to the authors of "original works of authorship," including literary, dramatic, musical, artistic, and certain other intellectual works (U.S. Copyright Office, 2008). This chapter will give examples of how authors are protected under copyright laws and how public domain and fair use allow users to copy published works.

Public Domain

Understanding public domain is important for educational leaders so no teacher or student violates these laws. Public domain is the body of all creative works and other knowledge. This includes writing, artwork, music, science, inventions, and other creative works—in which no person or organization has any proprietary interest. (Proprietary interest is typically represented by a copyright or patent.) Such works and inventions are considered part of the public's cultural heritage, and anyone can use and build upon them without restriction (not taking into account laws concerning safety, export, etc.) (Public Domain, 2010). Essentially, this means a work that is not protected by a copyright is in the public domain.

To determine if a published work is public domain, knowing the date when the work was published can identify if it is protected by copyright.

> If a work was published in the U.S. from 1923 through 1963, the work is likely in the public domain. Even though authors could extend protection of their works by filing a copyright renewal during the 28th year after the work was first published, many authors failed to file the renewal on time. For works published in the U.S. from 1964 through 1977, the copyright renewal is automatic. This means that works published during this time automatically receive 95 years of copyright protection. Finally, if works were published in the U.S. after 1977 copyright protection is for the life of the author plus 70 years after the date of his or her death. (Find Law, 2012)

Today most published works are protected by copyright so fair use is granted and is beneficial to users.

Fair Use

Understanding fair use is important for educational leaders so no teacher or student violates these laws. What is fair use? Fair use is a limitation and exception to the exclusive rights granted by copyright law to the author of a creative work. In the United States' copyright law, fair use is a doctrine that permits limited use of copyrighted material without acquiring permission from the rights holders. Examples of fair use include commentary, criticism, news reporting, research, teaching, library archiving, and scholarship. It provides for the legal unlicensed citation or incorporation of copyrighted material in another author's work under a four-factor balancing test (Fair Use, 2012).

According to Find Law (2012) fair use allows portions of copyrighted works to be used without permission from the owner. Fair use protects users from copyright infringements. The fair use doctrine permits anyone to use copyright works, without the owner's permission, in ways that are fundamentally equitable and fair (The Fair Use Network, 2007).

When examining copyright and terms of use within education administrators, teachers and students should familiarize themselves with areas that could be affected by copyright laws. The most common areas are classroom copyright and rights granted under copyright law.

First, what is classroom copyright? Fair use protects users if they are doing something for the greater good. An example of this would be teaching. Teachers and students use printed materials, text for use in multimedia projects, videos, videos for use in multimedia projects, videos for integration into video projects, illustrations and photographs, music for integration into multimedia/video projects, computer software, Internet, television, cable television, and film or filmstrip in their classrooms.

Under section 108 of the Copyright Act (1976) teachers may make multiple copies for classroom use. According to the Fair Use Guidelines for Educational Multimedia (Bakker, 2000), students may use text in multimedia projects and teachers may incorporate text into multimedia for teaching courses. In section 110 of the Copyright Act teachers may use videotapes, DVDs, and laser discs in their classrooms without restrictions of length, percentage, or multiple use. Materials may be copied for archival purposes or to replace lost, damaged, or stolen copies.

The following are best practices for educational leaders for understanding fair use. Fair Use Guidelines for Educational Multimedia states that illustrations and photographs of works may be used in their entirety but not more than 5 images by any one artist or photographer; from a collection of photographs, not more than 15 images or 10 percent or whichever is less. Up to 10 percent of a copyrighted musical composition may be reproduced, performed, and displayed as part of a multimedia program produced by an educator or student for educational purposes (Bakker, 2000). According to sections 107 and 108 of the Copyright Act if computer software or licensed software is purchased, software may be installed at home and at school and on multiple machines. Software may be copied for archival use to replace lost, damaged, or stolen copies. Software can be distributed to users via a network. The librarians may make archival copies (Educational Cyberplaygound website, 2006).

According to Fair Use Guidelines for Educational Multimedia, Internet images may be downloaded for student projects and sound files may be downloaded for use in projects. Congress states that live "of the air" broadcast may be used for instruction. Tapes made from broadcast may be used for instructions as well. Cable Systems (and their associations) state that cable television may be used with permission. Many programs may be retained for years depending on the program. Teachers may duplicate a single copy of a small portion of films or filmstrips for teaching purposes (Educational Cyberplaygound website, 2006).

Second, what are rights granted under copyright law? This section talks about the legal issues of creating a website. Tysver (2012) discusses five concerns when creating a website. The concerns are:

- copyright concerns
- domain name concerns
- trademark concerns
- defamationlinking
- framing.

When creating a web page obtaining images from the Web the creator should follow these five concerns. Create original images from drawing and painting programs. The creator should not take images from third parties. This can be an infringement of the creator's copyright. Licensed images from the Internet for example, Microsoft's Explorer logo may be copied as long as the copier accepts the terms of a license. Clip-art can be used from clip-art libraries provided with software. Free Images off the Internet can be used if some type of credit is given to the author. A web creator has no copyright concerns if text is developed by the creator and the original. Copyright violations can come into play if the creator of the website develops Java applets, Java scripts, and ActiveX scripts like text and pictures (pp. 1–2).

WEBSITE DOMAIN

When creating a website a domain name is one of the most important details. The domain name is the address for the website. The most common top-level domain names are .com, .org, .net, .gov, .edu. A whois search should be done to make sure the name is not taken and then a trademark search to make sure no one has chosen the domain name. If a name is available, a registration can be filed with InterNIC using their online registration form. To protect the domain name the owner should obtain a trademark registration.

A website usually has a trademark. A trademark is a slogan, word, or image that represents your organization. Website developers should be concerned with potential trademark issues. Potential issues can be: trademarks of others, linking to another page through that party's logo or trademark, selecting a trademark, and protecting a trademark through the federal trademark registration (Tysver, 2012).

According to Tysver (2012), webpage developers need to be careful to avoid defaming someone in their pages. If a statement is being made that may damage the reputation of a person or organization, care should be taken to make sure that the statement is not defaming. There are not many laws relating to the Internet on defamation. Finally, if a web developer plans to link or frame on their website great care needs to be taken. Consequently, one should not link to images found on another's party website without first getting permission. Frames in a website are used to subdivide web pages into parts. Problems can arise if a frame is used to show pages from two websites at the same time. Users can be misled by the content and issues may be raised of copyright infringement.

COPYRIGHT LAWSUITS

A lawsuit or (less commonly) "suit in law" is a civil action brought in a court of law in which a plaintiff, a party who claims to have incurred loss as a result of a defendant's actions, demands a legal or equitable remedy. The defendant is required to respond to the plaintiff's complaint. If the plaintiff is successful, judgment will be given in the plaintiff's favor, and a variety of court orders may be issued to enforce a right, award damages, or impose a temporary or permanent injunction to prevent an act or compel an act. A declaratory judgment may be issued to prevent future legal disputes.

PIVOTAL SOFTWARE LICENSING LAWSUIT

The following are some major U.S. software licensing cases that will give educational leaders perspective on the nature of recent court decisions. According to Geronimo, Nathan (IP Law Blog, 2011), Apple Inc., one of the largest software companies, sued Psystar Corp. for copyright infringement. Apple claimed that Psystar misused their software license agreement. Psystar initially made a master copy of Apple's Mac OS X operating software and then installed the software on their computers for sale to other retailers. In order to cover up their actions they packaged their computers with unopened versions of the operating software so that it may appear as if they had purchased the software to run on each individual computer it sold. The computers, however, actually ran on the preinstalled Mac OS X that was duplicated from the master copy Psystar originally made. Psystar's argument to this was the copyright misuse defense. According to Geronimo, Nathan (IP Law Blog, 2011), the copyright misuse defense was meant to deal with licensing agreements that impose unlawful restraints on the development and creation of competing software. This argument may have been effective if Apple Inc.'s License Agreement didn't state that:

> This License allows you to install, use and run one (1) copy of the Apple Software on a single-Apple-labeled computer at a time. You agree not to install, use or run the Apple Software on any non-Apple labeled computer, or to enable others to do so. (IP Law Blog 2011)

Every single one of those points (terms agreed upon) were violated. The U.S. Federal District Court ruled against Psystar on copyright infringement and copyright misuse. It was determined that Psystar violated Apple Inc.'s copyrights by its deceptive practices.

The following are some major U.S. copyright cases that will give educational leaders some perspective into the nature of recent court decisions. According to World Law Direct Forums (2009), 14 major companies were sued by Software Freedom Conservancy, Inc. (Erik Andersen) for copyright infringement by use of a software called BusyBox. The major companies involved were Best Buy Co., Inc., Samsung Electronics America, Inc., Westinghouse Digital Electronics, LLC, JVC Americas Corporation, Western Digital Technologies, Inc., Robert Bosch LLC, Phoebe Micro, Inc., Humax USA Inc., Comtrend Corporation, Dobbs-Stanford Corporation, Versa Technology Inc., Zyxel Communications Inc., Astak Inc., and GCI Technologies Corporation. The lawsuit against these companies accused them of distributing, ongoing copying, modifying, and/or distributing the copyrighted BusyBox software without permission;, even after several previously ignored attempts to notify them of their violations. The Conservancy acts as the corporate home and fiscal sponsor for various "free and open source software (FOSS)" projects (World Law Direct Forums, 2009). It also represents individual owners of copyrighs in their member projects. In this case, one of their owners, by the name of Erik Andersen, developed, marketed, distributed, and licensed the BusyBox computer software professionally. He's also the owner of the copyright to the computer software. This software consists of a set of computing tools and optimizes them for the use of computers with limited resources (such as cell phones, PDAs, and other small specialized electronics devices). Its source code (executable commands in a computer program) is also known to be very customizable, fast, and flexible and is used in many products sold around the world (World Law Direct Forums 2009). The defendants (companies being sued) sold electronic products, such as high definition televisions, digital video recorders, DVD players, video cameras, and wireless routers with firmware (installed or downloadable) that contained BusyBox or work thereof without permission. By not complying with License these companies lost the rights permitted by BusyBox to copy, modify, sublicense, and/or distribute the product under the License Agreement; which is

121

as a result terminated and voided. The United States District Court judged in ruling for the plaintiffs who won their case against the defendants. The prosecution against the defendants was not based solely on monitory compensation and legal fees but on other damages as well.

According to Karvets (2011), in May 2011, plaintiffs (music artists and filmmaker Alkiviades David) filed a lawsuit against CNET (defendant). The lawsuit accused CBS Interactive and CNET's publisher of massive copyright infringement by making a profit from online piracy (theft, illegal use of copyrighted material such as copying, reproducing, or distribution) and having distributed millions of copies of LimeWire on CNET's downloadable website since 2008, which would in turn account for 95 percent of the LimeWire downloads. To continue with the court proceedings the United States District Court judge Dale Fischer requested evidence of the existing pirated material, which was one of the initial requirements to the case. At a later date, the plaintiffs produced a mere compilation of six materials (far from 95 percent); one movie (*Fishtales* by Alkiviades David) and five music tracks ("She a Star" by Detron Bendross; "Run Da Yard" by Jeffrey Thompkins; "Topless" by Diamond Smith, Spectatcular Smith, Joseph Smith, and Emmanuel DeAnda; "Tipsy In Dis Clubby" by Diamond Smith, Spectatcular Smith, Joseph Smith, and Emmanuel DeAnda; "Sex Drive" by Dennis Round, which at the time were not yet granted a U.S. copyright registration (pending). At $150,000 in damages per work the plaintiffs were to receive approximately $900,000 plus legal fees if they prevailed in court. On July 4, 2011, Alkiviades David quietly withdrew his lawsuit. However, his lawyers (Adam Wolfson) may choose to re-file the case at a later date including more plaintiffs and thousands of songs and other copyrighted material. According to Karvets (2011), Lory Lybeck, a Washington state copyright lawyer, said the allegations against CNET were tougher sell, because CNET didn't run a file-sharing service; it just allowed users to download the peer-to-peer software (LimeWire). LimeWire, on the other hand, agreed to pay $105 million dollars to settle accusations from the recording industry stating that they committed a substantial amount of copyright infringements (Karvets, 2011).

CONCLUSION

The Internet has given many opportunities to those with published works. Works can be distributed faster and found easier. Because of technology, students, teachers, and administrators need to be aware of their rights to copy and use published works. We know now, based on decades of use in schools, on findings of hundreds of research studies, and on the everyday experiences of educators and students, technology can improve teachers' skills and knowledge, and improve school administration and management (NSBA, 2011). After examining research on public domain and fair use, this chapter provides for a greater awareness of what your rights as a teacher and administrator are on copyright.

The lawsuits previously discussed are the reason for the creation of the Stop Online Piracy Act (SOPA) and Protect IP Act (PIPA), which are to aid in the reduction or even possibly elimination of the illegal (unauthorized) copying, reproduction, and distribution of copyrighted material (intellectual property or work). Everyone has the right to be recognized or making a profit from their creative work. Theft, whether it is of creative work or physical property, is wrong and should be recognized as such. People should be aware of the harm this may cause. There are serious consequences of copyright infringement and illegal use of someone else's property for profit or gain. Business owners must be very careful with any material they decide to use and they must make sure that everyone at every level of their operation in the business knows the importance of respecting copyright material. Fortunately, the rules may sometimes be a little more flexible in the educational field. Many copyright owners may allow the use of their material for educational purposes (in expectation of future sales) but not for commercial use. Sometimes there is a requirement restricting the number of users or computers that may use the copyright material at a time. It is the responsibility of the school administrator to ensure that these rules are followed and that the proper training and awareness of the situation is administered. It is also important that an administrator understands that he/she should not assume their IT department knows about copyright laws because unfortunately this information is not taught to technicians at schools. As with everything, there should be checks and balances in place; make sure you protect your investment (school, business, or job).

QUESTIONS

1. How is fair use fair?

2. Can a person copy copyright software?

3. How do copyright laws affect students, teachers, and schools?

VIGNETTE CHAPTER 14   Fundraisers

Deep Creek High School is located in a close-knit mountain community. There are 1208 high school students at the school. There is a high graduation rate and active parent and community support for all school functions.

Mike Hughes is the band and music director and the senior class advisor. He is loved by students and parents. Under his direction, the band has won awards every year. He has been at Deep Creek High School for 15 years and is a graduate of the school. He is also the manager of the baseball team.

Deep Creek High School was gearing up to celebrate their annual Spring Carnival with local Fire Company #13. It is the biggest week-long event in the county, and everyone comes. There are tables to rent for craft vendors and spaces to rent for food and beverage vendors. Parking and admission are always free. The school clears around $18,000 each year, and the Fire Company clears about $45,000. The funds come from Bingo, 50/50 raffle tickets, a chance to win a car, pony rides, and a variety of contests.

This year Mike Hughes wanted to raise money for the prom decorations. He met with students from the 12th grade to brainstorm ideas for fundraising. They decided to create a music DVD to sell at the school's Spring Carnival. Throughout the school year, the Photography Club takes photos of students to include in the yearbook. Mike Hughes and his committee of students wanted to obtain photos and videos from the Photography Club to create a DVD showcasing the school and students. They expected that every parent would want to buy at least one DVD and hoped to raise about $5000 for prom decorations.

The technology was present in the school, the students were willing, and the Photography Club members agreed to share the video and photos with the Carnival as long as they got some funds for new equipment. Mr. Hughes asked his students what songs were really popular and had PG-13 language. He wanted to follow school policy on explicit material and language. Next he went to a paid download site and signed up to download music at $10 a month for one month, giving him rights to possess that music legally. The songs were selected and downloaded, the videos were edited, and photos were arranged and choreographed with music.

They created a cover for the DVD with the principal standing under the U.S. flag at the entrance of the school. When several copies were completed, Mr. Hughes showed the principal and teachers at the faculty meeting. He shared his fundraising plan and the amount of money he projected the students would raise with DVD sales. Mr. Hughes won full support of the faculty and administration. The students reproduced the music DVD 1000 times. The overhead cost to buy blank DVDs was low.

The week of the Spring Carnival came, and the students selected a booth near the entrance with hopes of having many customers. The DVDs were sold out in less than five days. As a result of the additional funds, the prom was a great success and a memorable night for the senior class.

Two months later, the school district's attorney received a lawsuit claiming damages by way of lost profits for representatives of the original music and the company Mr. Hughes paid to obtain the music. The suit claimed that Deep Creek High School reproduced copywritten materials without consent and profited from resale of that property. Additionally, the suit claimed that the label on the cover with the principal under the flag was also in violation of copyright laws and named the principal in the suit as a responsible party. The lawsuit estimated damages to be over $1 million.

QUESTIONS

1. Describe your school policy on copyright materials.

2. Discuss your understanding of copyright and fair use as it applies to school faculty.

3. Research or craft a new policy addressing fair use and copyright materials for your school.

ACTIVITY

1. In small group discussions identify from the list of stakeholders below the individuals that are affected by the dilemma in the vignette and brainstorm ways they can affect change.

2. How do they communicate and in what forum?

3. Discuss your school or district's written plan of action for this problem, if one exists.

4. Identify any resources that could be utilized to resolve this dilemma.

5. Have one person in your group take notes and share your group's findings in front of the class after the discussion.

6. Organize the consensus.

Outside Government Agencies	Outside Technology Professionals
Parents	Crisis Team
Principals	Outside Private Agencies
Staff	School Lawyers
Students	Counselor
Superintendent	School Board
Teachers	Media (TV, Radio, Internet)
Technology Personnel	State's Attorney

Glossary

Acceptable use policy: A series of guidelines that keep both the user and the organization informed about what expectations and actions are acceptable and what are not. It is the disclaimer releasing the school or industry from user wrongdoing and a guide for employee electronic equipment usage. This policy is a set of rules governing the usages of computers and related technologies. It is vital to the security of the organization that these rules be adhered to for the protection of organizational data.

Access policy: A policy designed to inform employees of the organization's expectations so that they can govern themselves in a professional manner. The purpose of these policies is to provide support to employees through the use of technology; therefore, anyone who utilizes the Internet or district's technology systems must foster that purpose by using Internet resources only for educational purposes and in an appropriate and legal manner. The organization must take steps to protect data with internal access policies insuring specific access limitations.

Act of bullying: Behavior consistent with physical or verbal abuse directed towards a person. Physical acts include hitting, pushing, kicking, or throwing objects at the victim. Verbal abuse, however, is consistent with taunting, cursing, name-calling, as well as subtle or indirect actions, such as social isolation and rumor-spreading about the individual(s). To compare the traditional bullying concept with electronic bullying; unlike traditional bullying, perpetrators can remain virtually anonymous using email systems, chat rooms, instant messaging, and other Internet venues hiding their identity to avoid personal contact with the victim(s).

Analysis policy: A policy that constitutes following predetermined technology standards to maintain the security of a system's infrastructure from outside threats. Analysis policy requires system administrators to be attentive to both internal and external threats. In order to keep the data protected with routine maintenance and monitoring of open network ports this should include: TCP packets, Operating System Hardening, router security and firewall maintenance. Additionally encryption development, network address translation, intrusion detection/prevention systems, and virus/Malware protection should also occur.

Auditing policy: A policy for examining, securing, and protecting data. Safeguarding the technology developed by the local education agency (LEA) should be included in the LEA's auditing policy and procedure. There are several software companies that can help provide various levels of data protection, however internal data protection audits can greatly reduce the chances of lost or stolen data. The auditing policy is the most complex as it examines compliance, organizational hardware and software lists, access lists, security concerns, and various other complicities of an organization's cyber security hardening.

Authentication policy: A policy designed for authorization, identification, and authentication control that ensures that only known system users make use of information systems and data access. It maintains authentication through secure socket layers, the use of ciphers, encryption, and recognized site certificate for access.

Backdoor: An unauthorized entrance into an organization's computer network via an open network port allowing authorization without identification or authentication.

Biometrics: An existing technology utilizing fingerprint recognition or eye retina software to capture a digital photograph and retrieve his/her information from a central console or program matching the unique characteristics with a number of identifying compatible points.

CAI (computer-assisted instruction): Computer programs that provide students with drill-and-practice exercises or tutorial programs.

CEI (computer-enhanced instruction): Instructions that provide less structured, more open-ended opportunities that support a particular lesson or unit plan. Use of the Internet, word processing, graphing, and drawing programs are examples of CEI.

Cipher: A shared mathematical formula allowing network or computer authorization via identification and authentication.

CMI (computer-managed instruction): Programs that evaluate and diagnose students' needs, guide them through the next step in their learning, and record their progress for teacher use.

Copyright law: In the United States this is based on the Copyright Act of 1976, a federal statute that went into effect on January 1, 1978. The Copyright Act prevents the unauthorized copying of a work of authorship. Copyright is a form of protection provided by the laws of the United States (title 17, U.S. Code) to the authors of "original works of authorship," including literary, dramatic, musical, artistic, and certain other intellectual works. This protection is available to both published and unpublished works.

Data protection: An organization's data is confidential and sensitive. Data should be stored on site, or off site, or in a secured central location. Data protection is necessary to maintain the integrity of the organization, and the information of all stakeholders. Internal data protection audits can greatly reduce the chances of lost or stolen data.

Data storage devices: Data storage mediums that can transfer data from one medium to another with direct connectivity. These devices are small and have a large storage capacity and high data-transfer rates.

Disaster recovery: A plan to recover and maintain the integrity of an organization's data for continued operation.

Download: Data transferred from one medium to another via the Internet or a data storage device.

Electronic bullying: The use of information and communication technologies to support, deliberate, repeated, and hostile behavior by an individual or group that is intended to harm others. However, cyber bullying subsequently is when students used the Internet, cell phone, along with other devices to send or post text or images intended to hurt or humiliate others.

Electronic sexual harassment: A term referring to the use of electronic devices to harass, torture, or physically harm a person in a sexual manner via computers, cell phones, iPads, emails, and social networks.

Encryption: A shared unique mathematical formula allowing network or computer authorization via identification and authentication.

Explicit materials: Any and all materials that are deemed offensive to a group or individual and described within the acceptable use policy. Any and all materials found to be of an explicit nature by federal, state, or local laws and ordnances.

Fair use: A limitation and exception to the exclusive rights granted by copyright law to the author of a creative work. In the United States Copyright Law, fair use is a doctrine that permits limited use of copyright material without acquiring permission from the rights holders.

Filters (sometimes referred to as border managers): Software designed to prevent access to the network. They identify unwanted materials through key words and phrases and prevent access. Filters must be updated and maintained regularly.

Firewall: A software system with an access control list preventing access without authorization via identification and authentication. Routine firewall system maintenance is required to maintain a secure system. Additionally, firewall and access control lists (ACLs) create an automated system that changes passwords on a periodic basis, make passwords complex utilizing numbers, letters, and symbols, and encrypt sensitive network traffic by using Secure Shell or Secure Network Management Protocol encryption.

Frozen workstations: Computer workstations loaded with software restricting configuration changes. This software is password protected and allows the computer to return to its default settings.

Idle configuration: A state of idleness where a computer is logged on but no one is using it.

Internet-usage policy: A statement designed to make distinctions between official uses and discourage personal misuse in the organizational environment.

Internet-use policy: A legal document designed to inform employees of appropriate use and professional conduct while using the Internet system. There are many complex components in the Internet-Usage Policy that determines its impact on the culture of the organization. These components include: downloading, utilizing filters, video streaming, popup, advertising rules, email usage, and other organizational rules.

Intrusion detection: Software that identifies an unrecognized authorization via not providing the requested identification for authentication while performing the seven-layer exchange.

IP security: Internet protocol security identifies only TCP/IP transmission control protocol/Internet protocol transmissions. It is a set of Internet rules governing transmission of data.

Malware: A malicious unauthorized intrusion software program like Trojan Horses, Spyware, and Adware that attaches to the transfers for files and folders and slows performance.

Media streaming: Streaming and buffered media such as video or music via downloading from a source host.

Network access logons: Assigned individual complexities identifiers needing a matching password for access.

Network address translation (NAT): A system that modifies the network IP address information while it is in transit through the system routers. NAT translates personal system address information to a public address that represents the company-wide address and hides all internal IP address information.

Network ports: Passageways, openings, or doorways through which applications on a systems computer can reach the software on a system server. Web pages and data transfer software require their respective ports to be "open" on the system's Internet server in order to be publicly accessible. The standard port for http or Internet web page access is port 80. The standard port for email access is port 25.

OS Hardening: The acronym stands for Operation System Hardening. It dictates that protecting the operating system requires system administrators to install and maintain updates and service patches as required.

Password complexities: Passwords requiring a mixture of uppercase letters, lowercase letters, numbers, and characters.

Physical policy: A set of rules governing the secure physical access to network equipment, network data, individual computers, storage devices, and company data.

Point-to-Point Tunneling Protocol: A rule allowing two main encrypting processes to include IPsec which encrypts data at the packet level and Point-to-Point Tunneling Protocol which encrypts information over virtual private networks or intranets.

Pop-ups: Programs designed to stream or download additional viewable web pages.

Privacy policy: A legal document or disclaimer that discloses and manages a customer's or employee's data, personal information, or professional identification. All privacy policies are different dependent upon the organization or industry. The privacy policy intends to protect all important and personal information related to an employee or customer.

Public domain: The body of all creative works and other knowledge—this includes writing, artwork, music, science, inventions, and other creative works—in which no person or organization has any proprietary interest. Proprietary interest is typically represented by a copyright or patent.

Remote access: Access is gained to another computer located anywhere, and from a different terminal, to perform administrative and routine tasks.

Router: A computer designed to be a network gateway to the Internet and protection from intrusion. It acts by address routing two-way transmissions using Transmission Control Protocol/Internet Protocol.

Sex texting (also known as sexting): The sending of sexually explicit photographs or messages via mobile phone.

Sexual harassment: Persistent and unwanted sexual advances, typically in the workplace, where the consequences of refusing are potentially very disadvantageous to the victim. Sexual harassment has been around for decades but, within the past 5 years with technology advancing, sexual harassment has advanced into electronic sexual harassment.

Site certificate: A certification of authorization, identification, and authentication that ensures that only known users with certified site certificates are allowed into an information system.

TCP (Transmission Control Protocol) packets: Transmission which consists of all the information being transferred including a header, the part that identifies the sender in the seven-layer Open Systems Interconnection model. Being able to analyze the information in the packets reveals where the data is coming from and can assist in preventing harmful data from entering the network.

TCP/IP (Transmission Control Protocol/Internet Protocol): Data transfer rules governing computer usage of the Internet.

Total Cost of Ownership (TCO): A comprehensive set of methodologies, models, and tools to help organizations better measure, manage, and reduce costs and improve overall value of IT investment. The TCO analysis for direct and indirect costs include the following elements: commissioning costs, conversion costs, disposal costs, downtime costs, energy costs, financing costs, installation costs, maintenance costs, productivity costs, purchase price, repair costs, risk costs, safety costs, service costs, support costs, training costs, and upgrade costs.

Virus: A computer programs that is designed to destroy and disrupt data and software programs on the computer or server.

Website domain: The address for the website. The most common top-level domain names are: .com, .org, .net, .gov, .edu. If a name is available, a registration can be filed with InterNIC using their online registration form. To protect the domain name the owner should obtain a trademark registration.

Wireless access: A device that allows wireless devices to connect to a wired network using Wi-Fi, Bluetooth, or other related standard wireless equipment from what is known as a hotspot or access point.

References

PREFACE

Chaika, Glori (August 16, 1999). Technology in the schools: It does make a difference! *Education World*. Retrieved from http://www.education-world.com/a_admin/admin122.shtml

Chaika, Glori (August 16, 1999). Technology in the schools: Some say it doesn't compute! *Education World*. Retrieved from http://www.education-world.com/a_admin/admin121.shtml

Exploring radical visions for tomorrow's schools (2010) Retrieved from http://www.oecd.org/dataoecd/43/0/45943716.pdf

Gabriel, K. D. (2007). *Ezine articles, future trends for education in America*. Retrieved from http://ezinearticles.com/?Future-Trends-for-Education-in-America&id=1105641

Lohman, J. (2010). *Comparing NCLB and RTTT*. Retrieved from http://www.cga.ct.gov/2010-R-0235.htm

MacKinnon, S. (2003, January–March). *TechKnowLogia*. Retrieved from http://www.techknowlogia.org/TKL_Articles/PDF/463.pdf

Rand, Critical Technologies Institute Annual Report: 1995–1996 Retrieved from http://www.rand.org/pubs/annual_reports/AR7005/index2.html

Standerfer, L. (2006). Before NCLB: The history of ESEA. *Principal Leadership*, 6(8), 26–27.

U.S. Department of Education (2010). Homeroom. Retrieved from http://www.ed.gov/blog/2010/10/building-skills-for-america%E2%80%99s-future

Warlick, D. (2005). *The future of education*. Retrieved from http://davidwarlick.com/connectlearning/?p=52

Webster Dictionary. (2012). Change. Retrieved from http://www.merriam-webster.com/dictionary/change

1 INTRODUCTION

Amos, D. (September 2003). Will technology divide us? Science and technology. *ABC News*. Retrieved from http://www.more.absnews.go.com/sections/scitech/rev_haves1125

Bennett, J. (December 2003). National educational technology standards: Raising the bar by degrees. *Infotoday*. Retrieved from http://www.infotoday.com/default.shtml

Brewster, C., & Klump, J. (2005). *Leadership practices of successful principals*. Northwest Regional Educational Laboratory. Portland, Oregon. *Educational Leadership Preparation*, 4(1), 1–4.

Gray, D. (2009). A new look at instructional leadership. *International Journal of Humanities and Social Science*. Retrieved from www.ijhssnet.com/journals/Vol_2_No_13_July_2012/6.pdf

Gunter, H. (2001). Critical approaches to leadership in education. *Journal of Educational Enquiry*, 2(2), 94–108.

Hallinger, P. (2003). Leading educational change reflections on the practice of instructional and transformational leadership. *Cambridge Journal of Education*, 33(3), 329–351.

Hopkins, D. (2001). Instructional leadership and school improvement. *National College for School Leadership*, 1–7. Retrieved from http://www.ncsl.org.uk

Howard, S., & Pope, M. (2002). Technology integration: Closing the gap between what preservice teachers are taught to do and what they can do. *Journal of Technology and Teacher Education*, 10(2). Retrieved from http://aace.org/dl/index.cfm/fuseaction/ViewPaper/id/9223/toc/yes

Interstate School Leaders Licensure Consortium. (2008). Educational leadership policy administration. Washington, DC: The Council of Chief State School Officers.

Johnson, C. (2001). *Meeting the ethical challenges of leadership: Casting light or shadow* Thousand Oaks, CA: Sage Publications.

Kirkpatrick, H., & Cuban, L. (Summer 1998). Computers make kids smarter—right? *Techno Quarterly*, 7(2). Retrieved from http://www.technos.net/tq_07/2cuban.htm

Kruger, M., Witziers, B., & Sleegers, P. (2007, March). The impact of school leadership on school level factors: Validation of a causal model. *School Effectiveness and School Improvement*, 18(1), 1–20.

Marturano, A., & Gosling, J. (2008). *Leadership: The key concepts*. New York, NY: Routledge.

National Association of Elementary School Principals. (2008). *Leading learning communities: Standards for what principals should know and be able to do*. Alexandria, Virginia.

Northouse, P. G. (2001). *Leadership: Theory and practice* (5th ed.). Thousand Oaks, CA: Sage Publications.

Offerman, L., Kennedy, J., & Wirtz, P. (1994). Implicit leadership theories: Content, structure, and generalizability. *Leadership Quarterly*, 5(1), 43–58.

Robinson, V. (2007). *The impact of leadership on student outcomes. Making sense of the shadow*. Thousand Oaks, CA: Sage Publications.

Stewart, J. (2006). Transformational leadership: An evolving concept examined through the works of Burns, Bass, Avolio, and Leithwood. *Canadian Journal of Educational Administration and Policy*, 54(26), 1–29.

U.S. Department of Education (2002) *Trends in International Mathematics and Science Study (TIMSS)* National Center for Education Statistics. Retrieved from http://nces.ed.gov/timss

Wise, A. (Fall 2003). A message to NCATE institutions board members, constituent organizations, and friends. *National Council for Accreditation of Teacher Education*. Retrieved from http://www.ncate.org

Wu, M. (2006). Compare participative leadership theories in three cultures. *China Media Research*, *2*(3), 19–30.

Yell, M., Drasgow, E., & Lowery, A. (2005). No child left behind and student with autism spectrum disorders. *Focus on Autism and Other Developmental Disorders*, *20*(3), 130–139.

2 TOTAL COST OF OWNERSHIP

Downloads | Publications. (2011, September 5). *Uptime institute*. Retrieved from http://uptimeinstitute.com/component/docman/cat_view/23-publications

Educase Center for Applied Research (ECAR). (2004). *Total Cost of Ownership: A strategic tool for ERP planning and implementation*. Retrieved from http://www.educause.edu/library/resources/total-cost-ownership-strategic-tool-erp-planning-and-implementation

Education – How much does it really cost to introduce and sustain computers in schools? (n.d.). *World Bank Group*. Retrieved from http://web.worldbank.org/WBSITE/EXTERNAL/TOPICS/EXTEDUCATION/0,,contentMDK:21956632~menuPK:617610~pagePK:148956~piPK:216618~theSitePK:282386,00.html

Emerging Education Technology. (2010, June 21). Let's stop misspending education technology dollars *EmergingEdTech. Education Technology. Internet and Instructional Technologies for Teachers & Other Educators*. Retrieved from http://www.emergingedtech.com/2010/06/lets-stop-misspending-education-technology-dollars

Gartner (2004). *Total cost of ownership schools*. Gartner Group Online. Retrieved from http://k12tco.gartner.com/home/default.aspx

Hoffman, T, (2003). *Gartner Group: Debunking five myths of TCO*. Retrieved from http://www.computerworld.com/s/article/82011/Gartner_Debunking_five_myths_of_TCO

Indirect-Cost Guidelines. (2010, May 20). *Indirect-cost guidelines*. Retrieved from http://www.gatesfoundation.org/grantseeker/Documents/Indirect Cost Policy.pdf

Total Cost of Ownership. (n.d.). *Wikipedia*. Retrieved from http://en.wikipedia.org/wiki/Total_cost_of_ownership

What is TCO (Total Cost of Ownership)? (2009, November 29). *Data Center Information, News and Tips – SearchDataCenter.com*. Retrieved from http://searchdatacenter.techtarget.com/definition/TCO

3 ACCEPTABLE USE POLICY

Dorchester County Public Schools. (2002). *Acceptable use policy*. Retrieved from http://www.dcps.k12.md.us/pdfs/I_policy07.pdf

Findlaw. (2011). *O'Connor v. Ortega*, 480 U.S. 709 (1987). Retrieved from http://caselaw.lp.findlaw.com/cgibin/getcase.pl?court=us&vol=480&invol=709

Fitzer, K. (2002). *Enforcing acceptable use policies*. Retrieved from http://www.ed.uiuc.edu/wp/crime-2002/aup.htm

iSAFE America Inc. (2011). *Acceptable use policies*. Retrieved from http://www.isafe.org/imgs/pdf/education/AUPs.pdf

Lightspeed Systems. (2010). *Acceptable use policies: Creating and enforcing guidelines for use of school technologies.* Retrieved from http://resources.lightspeedsystems.com/pdf/AUP_WP.pdf

Media Awareness. (2011). *Acceptable use policies for Internet use.* Retrieved from http://www.mediaawareness.ca/english/resources/special_initiatives/wa_resources/wa_teachers/backgrounders/acceptable_use.cfm

Meyer, L., & Johnson, E. H. (2011). *Preserving a CFAA claim when employee misappropriate data.* Retrieved from http://www.natlawreview.com/article/preserving-cfaa-claim-when-employees-misappropriate-data

Smith, B. W., Woodsum, D., & MacMahon, D. (1999). Legal *consideration in regulating employee use of school technology.* Portland, ME: United States District Court, District of Maine.

Standler, R. (2002). *Issues in a computer acceptable use policy.* Retrieved from www/rbs2/cp,/policy.htm

Tedford, T., & Herbeck, D.A. (2006). *Freedom of speech in the United States* (6th ed.). State College, PA: Strata Publishing, Inc.

U.S. Constitution (2011) A Hypertext version, U.S. Constitution Amend. I, U.S. Constitution Amend. IV, U.S. Constitution Amend. XIV. Retrieved from http://www.usconstitution.net/const.html

Virginia Department of Education (VDOE). (2011). *Acceptable use policy.* Retrieved from http://www.doe.virginia.gov/support/safety_crisis_management/internet_safety/acceptable_use_policy.shtml

Wentzell, B. (2001). *Writing an acceptable use policy for your school.* Retrieved from http://catnet.sdacc.org/resources/res_ID7.pdf

4 AUTHENTICATION POLICY

Authorization, Identification, and Authentication Policy Template. (2011). *Info Tech Research Group*, 1.

California Technology Assistance Project CTAP (2011). *Acceptable use policy articles.* Retrieved from http://www.myctap.org/index.php/cybersafety-home/68-acceptable-use-policy-articles

InfoTech (2011). Develop and deploy a security policy (PowerPoint) Retrieved from http://www.slideshare.net/Info-Tech/develop-security-policy

Kobus, W. (2007). *Identification and authentication policy.* Data Security Policies, 1. Security Manual. (2005). *DHHS Policies and Procedures*, 1–11.

Info-Tech Research Group (2011). *Authorization, Identification, and Authentication Policy Template.* Retrieved from http://www.infotech.com/research/authorization-identification-authentication- policy-template

University, S. (2006). Identification and authentication systems. *Administrative Guide Memo*, 1–4.

User Identification and Authentication. (2007). *Finjan Vital Security*, 1–46.

Vmware. (2011). Encryption and Authentication Policies. Retrieved from http://www.vmware.com/support/ace/doc/policies_enc_ace.html

5 INTERNET-USE POLICY

Arnesen, D. W., & Weis, W. L. (2007). Developing an effective company policy for employee Internet use and email use. *Journal of Organizational Culture, Communications and Conflict*, 1–4. Retrieved from jme.sagepub.com/content/34/3/342

Frankel, M., & Siang, S. (1999). Ethical & legal aspects of human subjects research on the Internet: A report of a workshop. *American Association for Advancement of Science-Directorate of Science & Policy Programs*, 1–25. Retrieved from http://www.aaas.org/spp/sfrl/projects/intres/report.pdf

Green, H., & Hannon, C., (2007). *Their space: Education for digital generation* (online version). Accessed September 4, 2007, from http://www.demos.co.uk/files/their%20space%20-%web.pdf

Hill, E. (2011). *Illegal file sharing at Elon, local universities: A look at policies and student awareness. Keeping up with what matters.* Retrieved from http://evahillreporting.wordpress.com/2011/04/28/illegal-downloading-at-elon-local-universities

Howard University. (2011). *Information systems & services*. Download Policy. Retrieved from http://www.howard.edu/technology/info/web/policy/mp3policy.htm

Norton, D. (2002). *Update your Internet use policy to stop download abuse.* Retrieved from http://www.techrepublic.com/article/update-your-internet-use-policy-to-stop-download-abuse/1039353

Project, D. E. (n.d.). *Monitoring computer & Internet use at work.* Retrieved from http://www.duke.edu/~hch2/cps1/DigitalEthics

SANS. (2011). *Information security policy templates.* Retrieved from http://www.sans.org/security-resources/policies

Stephenson, H. (2006, May 8). Employer concerns with growth increased of employee Internet use: Proquest. *Lawyer's Weekly USA*, 1.

6 ACCESS POLICY

Aberdeem Group (2012) Online Publication. Retrieved from http://www.docstoc.com/docs/110156383/Internet-Acceptable-Usage-Policy-Guidelines

Arnesen, D. W., & Weis, W. L. (2007). Developing an effective company policy for employee Internet use and email use. *Journal of Organizational Culture, Communications and Conflict*, 1–4.

Carswell, A., (2001) *Developing an effective company policy for employee Internet.* Retrieved from www.highbeam.com/doc/1G1-175110746.html

Digital Ethics Project (2012). *Monitoring computer & Internet use at work.* Retrieved from http://www.duke.edu/~hch2/cps1/DigitalEthics

Frankel, M., & Siang, S. (1999). Ethical & legal aspects of human subjects research on the Internet: A report of a workshop. *American Association for Advancement of Science— Carswell 2001 Directorate of Science & Policy Programs*, 1–25.

Green, H., & Hannon, C. (2007). Their space: Education for digital generation. Retrieved from http://www.demos.co.uk/files/their %20space%20-%web.pdf

Project, D. E. (n.d.). *Monitoring computer & Internet use at work.* Retrieved from http://www.duke.edu/~hch2/cps1/DigitalEthics

Robinson, S. (2010, November 2). *U.S. Information security law, part 1*. Retrieved from http://www.symantec.com/connect/articles/us-information-security-law-part-1

Stephenson, H. (2006, May 8). Employer concerns with growth increased of employee Internet use: Proquest. *Lawyer's Weekly USA*, 1.

Websense (2006) *Work related Internet*. Retrieved from http://infoacrs.com/wri/work.html

7 AUDITING POLICY

Bakia, M., Mitchell, K., & Yang, E., (2007). *State strategies and practices for educational technology: Volume I—Examining the enhancing education through technology program, U.S. Department of Education Office of Planning, Evaluation and Policy Development*. Retrieved from www.ed.gov/about/offices/list/opepd/ppss/reports.html

Conrad, B. (2010). Business security policies & procedures. *Small Business Chronicles*. Retrieved from http://smallbusiness.chron.com/business-secruity-policies-procedures-13739.html

Cradler, J., (1996) *Critical Issue: Developing a School or District Technology Plan*. Retrieved from http://www.ncrel.org/sdrs/areas/issues/methods/technlgy/te300.htm

Daintith, J. (2004). *Computer Misuse Act 1990. A dictionary of computing*. Retrieved from http://www.encuclopedia.com/doc/1011-ComputerMisuseAct1990

Delaware State University. (2011). *Acceptable use policy*. Retrieved from http:desu.edu.acceptable-use-Policy

Jeong, M. (n.d.). *Answers.com*. Retrieved from http://wiki.answers.com/Q/Why_computers-were-made

Jones, S., & Ball, A. (2008). The data framework: A first step in the data management challenge. *The International Journal of Digital Curation. 2*(3).

Missouri Department of Education (2011). *Department of elementary and secondary education*. Retrieved from http://dese.mo.gov/divimprove/instrtech/techplan/gettingstarted.htm

Office of Educational Technology (1994). *Critical issues: Developing a school or district technology plan*. Retrieved from http://www.ncrel.org/sdrs/areas/issues/methods/technlgy/te300.htm

Robinson, S. (2010, November 2). U.S. *Information security law, part 1*. Retrieved from http://www.symantec.com/connect/articles/us-information-security-law-part 1

SANS Institute. (2006). *Open directory project September 2011*. Retrieved from http:222.dmoz.org/computers/security/policy/sample_policies/html

8 PHYSICAL POLICY

Ask.com Encyclopedia. (2011, September 20). *Popular questions*. Retrieved from http://www.ask.com/wiki/Network_security

Conrad, B. (2010). Business security policies & procedures. *Small Business Chronicles*. Retrieved from http://smallbusiness.chron.com/business-secruity-policies-procedures-13739.html

Daintith, J. (2004). *Computer Misuse Act 1990. A dictionary of computing*. Retrieved from http://www.encyclopedia.com/doc/1011-ComputerMisuseAct1990

Delaware State University. (2011). *Acceptable use policy*. Retrieved from http:desu.edu. acceptable-use-Policy

Jeong, M. (n.d.). *Answers.com*. Retrieved from http://wiki.answers.com/Q/Why_ computers-were-made

Robinson, S. (2010, November 2). *U.S. Information security law, part 1*. Retrieved from http://www.symantec.com/connect/articles/us-information-security-law-part 1

SANS Insitute. (2006). *Open directory project*. Retrieved from http://222.dmoz.org/ computers/security/policy/sample_policies/html

U.S. Department of Agriculture (2011). *The USDA directives system*. Retrieved from http://www.ocio.usda.gov/directives

9 ANALYSIS POLICY

Chester, W. (2010, May). Top 5 Threat Protection Best Practices. *Sophos Systems*. Retrieved from http://www.sophos.com/medialibrary/Gated%20Assets/white%20 papers/sophostop5threatprotectionbestpracticeswpna.pdf

Critical Laptop or Computer Network Protection Very Best Practices | Dragonflyband. (n.d.). *Dragonflyband.com*. Retrieved from http://www.dragonflyband.com/critical-laptop-or-computer-network-protection-very-best-practices

Davis, D. (n.d.). Fundamentals: Five ways to secure your Cisco routers and switches | TechRepublic. Retrieved from http://www.techrepublic.com/blog/networking/ fundamentals-five-ways-to-secure-your-cisco-routers-and-switches/470

Disaster Recovery. (n.d.). *GFS Software*. Retrieved from http://www.gfs.com.br/en/ Products/Disaster_Recovery.htm

Eckstein, C. (n.d.). *SANS: Computer security training, network security research, InfoSec resources*. Retrieved from http://www.sans.org

Enterprise Support—Symantec Corp. (n.d.). *Symantec—antivirus, anti-spyware, endpoint security, backup, storage solutions*. Retrieved from http://www.symantec.com/ business/support/index?page=content

Jennifer, M. A. (2007, July 12). *Best practices: Server operating system security*. Retrieved from http://www.ca.com/files/industryanalystreports/best_practices_server_operating. pdf

Main Page—OWASP. (n.d.). Retrieved from https://www.owasp.org/index.php/ Main_Page

Musthaler, L. (2009, September 11). Top 5 best practices for firewall administrators. *Network World*. Retrieved from http://www.networkworld.com/newsletters/2009 /091409bestpractices.html

Sophos Security Topics. (2011). Top 5 threat protection. *Antivirus, endpoint, disk encryption, email and Web security | Sophos*. Retrieved from http://www.sophos.com/en-us/ security-news-trends/security-trends/top-5-threat-protection-best-practices.aspx

Top 5 best practices for firewall administrators. (n.d.). *Network World*. Retrieved from http://www.networkworld.com/newsletters/2009/091409bestpractices.html

10 PRIVACY POLICY

Agency, U. E. (2010). *Privacy policy*. Retrieved from http://www.epa.gov/privacy/policy/2151

Center, E. P. (2010). *The Privacy Act of 1974*. Retrieved from http://epic.org/epic/about.html#contact

Privacy Policy. (2011). Retrieved from http://en.wikipedia.org/wiki/Privacy_policy

Services, U. D. (2011). *The Privacy Act*. Retrieved from http://www.hhs.gov/foia/privacy/index.html

11 CYBER RISK ASSESSMENT CHECKLIST PROFILE AND QUESTIONNAIRE

Evers, J. (2006) *Computer crime costs $67 billion, FBI says*. Retrieved from http://news.cnet.com/Computer-crime-costs-67-billion,-FBI-says/2100-7349_3-6028946.html

Moore's Law. (1970). *Moore's Law*. Retrieved from http://www.mooreslaw.org

12 ELECTRONIC BULLYING

Couvillon, M., & Ilieva, V. (2011). Recommended practices: A review of schoolwide preventative programs and strategies on cyber bullying. *Preventing School Failure: Alternative Education for Children and Youth*, *55*(2), 96–101. doi: 10.1080/1045988X.2011.539461

Dictionary.com. (n.d.). Retrieved from http://dictionary.reference.com/browse/sexting

IP Law Blog (2011, October). *Geronimo, Nathan. Apple wins pivotal software licensing lawsuit*. Retrieved from http://www.theiplawblog.com/archives/333286-print.html

Kowalski, R. M., & Limber, S. P. (2007). Electronic bullying among middle school students. *Journal of Adolescent Health*, 22–30.

Leary, M., (2008). *National Center for the Prosecution of Child Abuse (NCPCA)*. Retrieved from http://www.law.edu/Fac-Staff/LearyM/

Lenhart, A. (2009, December 15). *Pew Research Center's Internet & American Life Project*. Retrieved from http://www.pewinternet.org

Logan, J. (2011, February 18). *Taylor & Francis Journals: Welcome*. Retrieved from http://www.tandf.co.uk/journals/titles/1045988X.asp

Long, J., & Caradine, J. (2010). Tips for school administrators on how to handle "Sexting." *Education Law Newsletter*, *23*.

Manzo, K. K. (2009). Administrators confront student 'Sexting.' *Education Week*, *28*, 13–16.

Masnick, M. (2010). California Court says online bullying is not protected free speech. Retrieved from http://www.techdirt.com/articles/20100319/05031118631

Nathan, L. (2009). *National Center for Missing and Exploited Children. Cyberbullying*. Retrieved from http://www.aasa.org/content.aspx?id=11652

Ostrager, B. (2010). Translating the law to accommodate today's teens and the evolution from texting to sexting. *Family Court Review*, *48*(4), 712–726.

Oxford Dictionaries Online. (n.d.). Retrieved from http://oxforddictionaries.com/definition/sexting?region=us&q=sexting

Pascoe, C. J. (2011). Resource and risk: Youth sexuality and new media use. *Sexuality Research & Social Policy*, *8*, 5–17.

Patchin, J., & Hinduja, S. (2010). Electronic-cyberbullying. *Cyberbullying Research Center*, 1–5. Retrieved from http://www.cyberbullying.us/Students_Guide_to_Personal_Publishing.pdf

Raskauskas, J. (2007). Involvement in traditional and electronic bullying among adolescents. *Developmental Psychology*, 564–575. Retrieved from http://psycnet.apa.org/journals/dev/43/3/564

Smith, P., Mahdavi, J., Carvalho, M., Fisher, S., Russell, S., & Tippett, N. (2008). Cyberbullying: Its nature and impact in secondary school pupils. *Journal of Child Psychology and Psychiatry*, 376–386.

Sole, S., (2012) Proposed law focuses on electronic bullying. This week community news. Retrieved from http://www.thisweeknews.com/content/stories/grovecity/news/2012/01/24/Proposed-law-focuses-on-electronic-bullying.html

Stavros, K., & Androniki, K. (2010). Cyber bullying: A review of the literature on harassment through the Internet and other electronic needs. *Family & Community Health*, 1–2.

Taylor, K. R. (2010). Unconditional punishment? *Principal Leadership*, *1*(S), 8–10.

Weiss, R., & Samenow, C. P. (2010). Smart phones, social networking, sexting and problematic sexual behaviors—a call for research. *Sexual Addiction & Compulsivity: The Journal of Treatment & Prevention*, *17*(4), 241–246.

Willard, N. (2010). School response to cyber bullying and sexting: The legal challenges. *Center for Safe and Responsible Internet Use*, 1–17. Retrieved from http://csriu.org/documents/documents/cyberbullyingsextinglegal_000.pdf

Wong-Lo, M., & Bullock, L. (2011). Digital aggression: Cyberworld meets school bullies. *Preventing School Failure: Alternative Education for Children and Youth*, *55*(2), 64–70. doi: 10.1080/1045988X.2011.539429

13 ELECTRONIC SEXUAL HARASSMENT

Agger, C., & Day, K., (2011). Accessible information prevention strategies related to student sexual harassment: A review of students harassing students. *The High School Journal*, (94), 77–78.

Blase, J., & Blase, J. (2002). The dark side of leadership: Teacher perspectives of principal mistreatment. *Educational Administration Quarterly*, *38*(5), 671–727. Retrieved from http://www.articlebrain.com/Article/Electronic-Sexual-Harassment/109487

Brackett, N., & Brackett, B. Sexual harassment. *Etools4Education*. Retrieved from http://www.online-distance-learning-education.com/article_info.php/articles_id/15

Cassidy, W., Jackson, M., & Brown, K. N. (2009). Sticks and stones can break my bones, but how can pixels hurt me? Sexual harassment. Retrieved from http://en.wikipedia.org/wiki/Electronic_harassment

Electronic Sexual Harassment. (2012, March 18). Retrieved from http://en.wikipedia.org/wiki/Electronic_harassment

Equal Rights Advocates. (2012). *Sexual harassment at school: Know your rights*. Retrieved from http://www.equalrights.org/publications/kyr/shwork.asp

Fetter-Harrott, A. (2010). *Staff-to-student sexual harassment*. Retrieved from http://www.districtadministration.com/article/staff-student-sexual-harassment

Fogarty, K. (2009). *Teens and sexual harassment: Making a difference*. Retrieved from http://edis.ifas.ufl.edu/fy850

Harassment. (2012). How can pixels hurt me?: Students' experiences with cyber-bullying. *School Psychology International*, *30*(4), 383–402. Retrieved from http://en.wikipedia.org/wiki/Privacy_policy

Hill, C., & Kearl H. (2011). *Crossing the line: Sexual harassment at school*. Retrieved from http://www.aauw.org/learn/research/upload/CrossingTheLine.pdf

Jansen. (2012). Electronic sexual harassment. *Educational Administration Quarterly*, *39*(2), 187–207.

Lee, V. E., Croninger, R. G., Linn, E., & Chen, X. (1996). The culture of sexual harassment in secondary schools. *American Educational Research Journal*, *33*, 383–417.

Maine's Governor's Children Cabinet. (2006). *Maine's best practice in bullying and harassment prevention: A guide for schools and communities*. Retrieved from http://www.maine.gov/cabinet/Bullying_000.pdf

Quinn, D. (2003). Legal issues in educational technology: Implications for school leaders *Educational Administration Quarterly* (April) *39*: 187–207. Retrieved from http://eaq.sagepub.com/content/39/2/187.full.pdf+html

Science Daily. (2008). Sexual harassment at school: More harmful than bullying. Retrieved from http://www.sciencedaily.com/releases/2008/04/080423115922.htm

Shane, R. D. (2009). Teachers as sexual harassment victims: The inequitable protections of Title VII in public schools. *Florida Law Review*. Retrieved from http://lawprofessors.typepad.com/files/teachersexualharassment.pdf

Whitted, K. S., & Dupper, D. R. (2005). Best practices for preventing or reducing bullying in schools. Retrieved from http://blueskieswellnessinc.com/PDF/Best-Practice-for-Prevention-of-Bullying.pdf

Young, E. L., & Ashbaker, B. Y. (2008). Students services: Addressing sexual harassment. *Principal Leadership*. Retrieved from http://www.nasponline.org/resources/principals/Sexual%20Harassment%20November%2008.pdf

14 BASICS OF COPYRIGHT AND FAIR USE

About.com (2012). *Fisher, Tim. Firmware*. Retrieved from http://pcsupport.about.com/od/termsf/g/firmware.htm

An introduction to fair use and other free expression rights. (2007). *The Fair Use Network*. Retrieved from web.archive.org/web/20070827194907/http://fairusenetwork.org/reference/freeexpip

Bakker, C., (2000) *Saying "Yes" instead of "No": Promoting the Fair Use Guidelines for educational multimedia*. Retrieved from http://www.infotoday.com/mmschools/may00/bakker.htm

Copyright Basics. (2008). *U.S. Copyright Office*, *1*, 1–12. Retrieved from www.copyright.gov

141

REFERENCES

Copyright Clearance Center (2012). *Copyright basics*. Retrieved from http://www. copyright.com/viewPage.do?pageCode=au174

Educational Cyberplaygound. (2006, May). *Copyleft-Copyright*. Retrieved from www. edu-cyberpg.com/teachers/copyrightlaw.html

Fair Use. (2012). *Wikipedia*. Retrieved from en.wikipedia.org

Fair Use Network (2007). *An introduction to fair use and other free expression rights*. Retrieved from web.archive.org/web/20070827194907/http://fairusenetwork.org/reference/ freeexpip

Find Law. (2012, February 26). *Fair use or public domain*. Retrieved from smallbusiness. findlaw.com/copyright/copyright-using/public-domain-vs-fairuse.html

Karvets, D. (2011, June). Massive copyright lawsuit against CNET shrivels. Retrieved from http://www.wired.com/threatlevel/2011/06/cnet-lawsuit-shrivel

Meadows, C. (2008). *Should second-hand book stores pay royalties?* Retrieved from http:// www.teleread.com/library/should-second-hand-book-stores-pay-royalties

National School Boards Association (NSBA). (2011, September 9). *Technology's impact on learning*. Retrieved from www.nsba.org/sbot/toolkit/tiol.html

Public Domain. (2010). *Word IQ*. Retrieved from www.wordiq.com

Radcliffe, M., & Brinson, D. (1999). *Copyright Law*. Retrieved from http://library. findlaw.com/1999/Jan/1/241476.html

IP Law Blog (2011, October). *Geronimo, Nathan. Apple wins pivotal software licensing lawsuit*. Retrieved from http://www.theiplawblog.com/archives/333286-print.html

Tysver, D. (2012, February 24). *BitLaw a resource on technology law*. Retrieved from www. bitlaw.com/internet/webpage.html

U.S. Copyright Office. *Copyright basics, Circular 1*. Retrieved from http://www. copyright.gov/circs/cir01.pdf

World Law Direct Forums (2009, December). *Forum administrator. 16 companies sued by the Software Freedom Law Center*. Retrieved from http://www.worldlawdirect.com/ forum/copyright-trademark-patent/32809-copyright-lawsuit-16-companies-sued-software-freedom-law-center.html

Index

Note: 'N' after a page number indicates a note; 't' indicates a table.